REA's Books *
They have rescued lo†

MW00978161

(a sample of the <u>hundreds of letters</u> REA receives each year)

❝Your books are great! They are very helpful, and have upped my grade in every class. Thank you for such a great product.❞
Student, Seattle, WA

❝Your book has really helped me sharpen my skills and improve my weak areas. Definitely will buy more.❞
Student, Buffalo, NY

❝Compared to the other books that my fellow students had, your book was the most useful in helping me get a great score.❞
Student, North Hollywood, CA

❝I really appreciate the help from your excellent book. Please keep up your great work.❞
Student, Albuquerque, NM

❝Your book was such a better value and was so much more complete than anything your competition has produced (and I have them all)!❞
Teacher, Virginia Beach, VA

(more on next page)

(continued from previous page)

"Your books have saved my GPA, and quite possibly my sanity. My course grade is now an 'A', and I couldn't be happier."
Student, Winchester, IN

"These books are the best review books on the market. They are fantastic!"
Student, New Orleans, LA

"Your book was responsible for my success on the exam. . . I will look for REA the next time I need help."
Student, Chesterfield, MO

"I think it is the greatest study guide I have ever used!"
Student, Anchorage, AK

"I encourage others to buy REA because of their superiority. Please continue to produce the best quality books on the market."
Student, San Jose, CA

"Just a short note to say thanks for the great support your book gave me in helping me pass the test . . . I'm on my way to a B.S. degree because of you !"
Student, Orlando, FL

Super Review™

All You Need to Know!

COMPUTER
NETWORKS

Randall Raus, M.S.
Computer Engineer and
Computer Science Consultant
Seal Beach, CA

Research & Education Association
Dr. M. Fogiel, Director
61 Ethel Road West
Piscataway, New Jersey 08854

SUPER REVIEW ™
OF COMPUTER NETWORKS

Printed in the United States of America

Library of Congress Catalog Card Number 00-130282

International Standard Book Number 0-87891-084-0

SUPER REVIEW is a trademark of
Research & Education Association, Piscataway, New Jersey 08854

WHAT THIS *Super* **Review** WILL DO FOR YOU

This **Super Review** provides all that you need to know to do your homework effectively and succeed on exams and quizzes.

The book focuses on the core aspects of the subject, and helps you to grasp the important elements quickly and easily.

Outstanding **Super Review** features:

- Topics are covered in logical sequence

- Topics are reviewed in a concise and comprehensive manner

- The material is presented in student-friendly language that makes it easy to follow and understand

- Individual topics can be easily located

- Provides excellent preparation for midterms, finals and in-between quizzes

- In every chapter, reviews of individual topics are accompanied by Questions **Q** and Answers **A** that show how to work out specific problems

- Written by professionals and test experts who function as your very own tutors

Dr. Max Fogiel
Program Director

CONTENTS

Introduction

In the 1960s when multi-user timesharing systems were being implemented for the first time, the operator would type at what is referred to in computer jargon as a "dumb" terminal (a terminal with no computing power). These early systems allowed the user, whether local or remote, to have "virtual access" (giving each user the impression of direct access) to system resources by using a communications system or network that was basically "transparent" to the user.

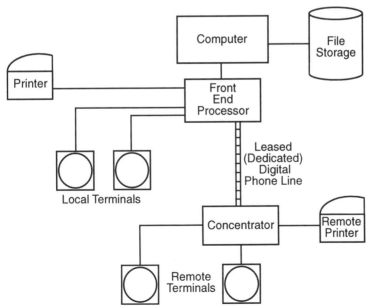

Fig. 1 Early Time Sharing System with a Hierarchical Tree Topology

These early systems were connected in a *hierarchical tree topology,* as shown in Fig. 1 on the previous page, and the terminal nodes operated in a master-slave relationship with the computer. The *concentrator,* in Fig. 1, is a device with limited processing and storage capability, that can accept data from a number of different devices and output it on a single line, and can also reverse the process, accepting data on a single line and outputting it to the appropriate device. The *leased (dedicated) phone line,* in this diagram, is shown to be digital; thus a modem is not required. Interestingly enough, AT&T was already offering what was called *digital data service* (DDS) as an option for computer communications by the early 1960's. The *front-end processor* is a special type of concentrator that is installed on the same site as the *host* computer. The main point of Fig. 1 is that the topology, processing power, and control of these early systems was hierarchical, with the terminals operating in a master-slave relationship with the host computer over a transparent communications system.

As the industry matured, a wide range of computers became available, from "intelligent" terminals, to minicomputers, to powerful mainframes capable of supporting hundreds of users simultaneously. Large organizations with many branches found they had reason to transfer information between branch offices more often. However, the master-slave hierarchy endured for a surprisingly long time. Even if two mainframes wanted to communicate, one would have to revert to slave status to accept data.

When personal computers appeared on the market and began to blossom on desktops everywhere because of their relatively low cost, people wanted to send and receive data from their PCs to mainframes. But PCs could only communicate with mainframes if they pretended to be dumb terminals. Some users resorted to printing out data from mainframes and typing it into their PCs. Other users wrote special programs to allow communication with mainframes.

Both options were awkward and inefficient at best, and a solution had to be found. It wasn't long before the most logical solution became apparent. This was a type of communication called *peer-to-peer com-*

munication between two *peer* entities. Either computer, regardless of its processing power could start, stop, or control communication.

The trend toward peer-to-peer communication has led to what is called *distributed network systems.* Modern computer networks are distributed, with processing power, data, and control distributed throughout the network. The PC, whether connected to a *local area network* (LAN) with other PCs, or, as has increasingly been the case, connected to a network with computers of a range of sizes, is seen as an intelligent workstation with access to a wide range of system resources.

As computer networks became increasingly complex interconnections between "heterogeneous" computers, often manufactured by different vendors, there were more and more calls for "plug-compatible" or "open systems." The only cost-effective way to allow heterogenous computers to interface, particularly across a wide geographic area, is to develop *standards* and *protocols* (protocols are the rules of communication). In fact, much of the study of computer networks is the study of standards and protocols.

Organizations which recommend, sanction, and document standards have played an extremely important role in the evolution of data communications and computer networks. These national and international standards bodies interact with each other in complex ways. For example, the Computer Society of IEEE (The Institute of Electrical and Electronics Engineers) may develop and publish a new standard, which then becomes accepted by The American National Standards Institute (ANSI). ANSI may then submit it to the International Organization of Standards (IOS), which may make minor modifications before enshrining it as an international standard. Fig. 2 (on next page) shows the major standards organizations and how they relate to each other.

In this book, we will describe the basics or essentials of the technologies that are used to implement a wide range of networks, from LANs to *wide area networks* (WANs), and to international networks such as the *Integrated Services Digital Network* (ISDN) and the *Internet.* Despite rapidly advancing technology, there is a core set of concepts

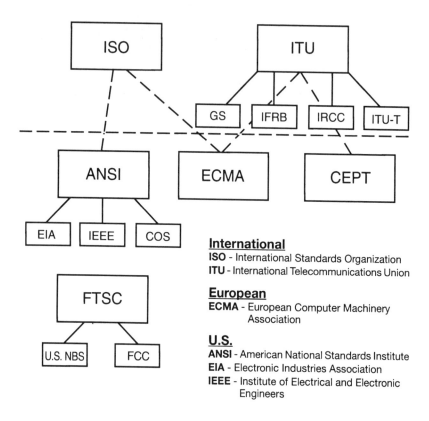

Fig. 2 International, European, and U.S. Standards Organizations

that remain constant, and it is this core set of concepts that is essential for the computer science student to learn in order to understand how computer networks work and to easily and quickly grasp new technological developments as they occur.

CHAPTER 1

Network Architecture

Network architecture is an abstract concept. It is also an important one. First, in Section 1.1, we will develop the concept of a protocol, because protocols are important building blocks of network architectures. In fact, a network architecture is sometimes defined as a *system of protocols*. In Section 1.2 we will describe network topologies and show how they relate to network architectures. In Section 1.3 we will explain the ISO's recommended *Open System's Interconnection* (OSI) *Reference Model* and show how it relates to the Berkley UNIX system that was created at the request of the defense department's Advanced Research Project Agency (ARPA) by the University of California at Berkeley in the early 1980's. Finally, we will give a more rigorous and complete definition of computer network architecture.

1.1 Protocols

A communications protocol is a set of rules for establishing communication and transmitting information between two or more entities on a communications network. Individual messages are called *protocol data units* (PDUs). A protocol specifies the rules and procedures for:

1. Establishing a connection (optional)
2. Node to node transmission of PDUs
3. Error control
4. *Forwarding* of PDU's at intermediate nodes (if end-nodes are not directly linked)

5. *Routing* of PDU's (if more than one route is possible)
6. Flow control to avoid congestion (optional)
7. Terminating or clearing a connection (if a connection was established
8. Other rules of communication

In Section 1.1.1 we will describe codes that are used to transmit information contained in PDUs. In Section 1.1.2 we will give a brief description of *Kermit,* which is a simple communication protocol. In Section 1.1.3 we will discuss another protocol, High-level Data Link Control (HDLC), which is widely used in computer networks.

1.1.1 Coding

While protocols provide the procedures and rules for data transfer, transmission codes are the language into which the data is transformed. Two commonly used transmission codes are the *Extended Binary Coded Decimal Interchange Code* (EBCDIC), which is a *de facto* standard used on IBM mainframes, and the *American Standard Code for Infor-*

Bits 4 to 7 First Hex Digit (MSB)

HEX	0	1	2	3	4	5	6	7	8	9	A	B	C	D	E	F
0	NUL	DLE			SP	&							(	)	\	0
1	SOH	SBA							a	j	-		A	J	S	1
2	STX	EUA		SYN					b	k	s		B	K		2
3	ETX	IC							c	l	t		C	L	T	3
4									d	m	u		D	M	U	4
5	PT	NL							e	n	v		E	N	V	5
6			ETB						f	o	w		F	O	W	6
7			ESC	EOT					g	p	x		G	P	X	7
8									h	q	y		H	Q	Y	8
9		EM							i	r	z		I	R	Z	9
A					¢	!	:									
B				.	$	,	#									
C	FF	DUP		RA	<	#	%	@								
D		SF	ENQ	NAK	(	)	-	'								
E		FM			+	;	>	=								
F		ITB		SUB	|	—	?	*								

Table 1.1 EBCDIC Character Set

Bits 0 to 3 Second Hex Digit (LSB)

mation Interchange (ASCII), which is sanctioned by ANSI. Table 1.1 (on previous page) shows the hexadecimal values for EBCDIC and Table 1.2 shows the hexadecimal values for ASCII.

Bits 4 to 6
First Hex Digit (MSB)

HEX	0	1	2	3	4	5	6	7
0	NUL	DLE	SP	0	a	P	`	p
1	SOH	DC1	!	1	A	Q	a	q
2	STX	DC2	•	2	B	R	b	r
3	ETX	DC3	#	3	C	S	c	s
4	EOT	DC4	$	4	D	T	d	t
5	ENQ	NAK	%	5	E	U	e	u
6	ACK	SYN	&	6	F	V	f	v
7	BEL	ETB	'	7	G	W	g	w
8	BS	CAN	(	8	H	X	h	x
9	HT	EM	)	9	I	Y	i	y
A	LF	SUB	*	:	J	Z	j	z
B	VT	ESC	+	;	K	[	k	{
C	FF	FS	,	<	L	\	l	|
D	CR	GS	.	=	M	]	m	}
E	SO	RS		>	N	-	n	–
F	SI	US	/	?	O	—	o	DEL

(Row labels at left: Bits 0 to 3 / Second Hex Digit (LSB))

Table 1.2 ASCII Character Set

The ASCII character set defines the characters with hexadecimal values 00H through 1FH as unprintable characters. Although the LF (line feed), CR (carriage return), and FF (form feed) characters will obviously have an effect when output to a printer or monitor, most of the ASCII characters in the range 00H to 1FH are control characters used in data transmission. Typical communication codes available in both ASCII and EBCDIC include the following:

SOH : *Start of Header* - used as the first character of a message, or PDU, and usually followed by other control characters (the header) and then the data field.

STX : *Start of Text* - used to indicate the beginning of the data field.

ETX : *End of Text* - used to indicate the end of the transmission field.

ETB : *End of Transmission Block* - used to indicate the end of a transmission block. When used in place of an ETX, it means not just the end of data for this message, but also for a block of messages containing data.

EOT : *End of Transmission* - used for line turnaround in half-duplex mode (which will be explained later).

ACK : *Positive Acknowledgment* - means data was received without error.

NAK : *Negative Acknowledgment* - indicates to the sender that data received was in error, and that a retransmission is requested.

We will concentrate on ASCII because it is more commonly used than EBCDIC. ASCII uses the rightmost seven bits of each byte to represent 128 characters including the letters of the alphabet, the ten decimal digits, punctuation marks, and the control characters shown in Table 1.2. The leftmost, or most significant bit of each byte can be used as a *parity bit* for error detection.

If *odd parity checking* is used, the parity bit is set to a 1 if the first seven bits contain an even number of 1s, otherwise it is cleared to 0. If *even parity checking* is used, the parity bit is set to a 1 if the first seven bits contain an odd number of 1s. The parity bit is set prior to transmission by the sending device. Upon reception, the receiving device checks if the parity bit has the correct value.

Because telephone lines and cables usually only allow transmission over a single line, the ASCII characters must be transmitted in *serial* form as shown in Fig. 1.1.

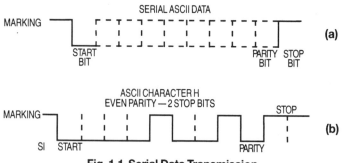

Fig. 1.1 Serial Data Transmission

Serial data transmission begins by lowering the voltage on the transmission line for a specified time period (the start bit in Fig. 1.1). Next, the parity bit is transmitted (if parity is used), followed by the character bits. Then the signal voltage is raised for one or two bit periods [the stop bits in Fig. 1.1 (a) and Fig. 1.1 (b)]. After that, the transmitter can then transmit the next character, by lowering the signal (the start bit again) or idle by keeping the signal high.

This is known as *asynchronous transmission* because the clocks on the sending and receiving devices are independent and only synchronized with each character (we will explain more about asynchronous and *synchronous transmission* in Chapter 2, The Physical Layer).

One of the ways ASCII characters are transmitted between computers is with the use of the *RS-232 interface,* which is a standard recommended by The Electronic Industries Association (EIA). The RS-232 interface consists of a 25 pin connector called a DB-25, a cable, a set of electrical characteristics, and a function description of each pin (we will examine the RS-232 and similar interfaces in more detail in Chapter 3). The RS-232 can also be used with a simplified 9-pin connector called a DB-9. Fig. 1.2 shows the pin numbers and nomenclature of a possible arrangement for using an RS-232 cable with a DB-9 and a DB-25 connector to connect two computers.

The RS-232 interface is usually used to connect a computer with a

DB - 9			DB - 25
Function	Pin No.	Pin No.	Function
Received Data	2 ←—	3	Transmitted Data
Transmitted Data	3 —→	2	Received Data
Data Terminal Ready	4 ←—	6	Data Set Ready
Ground	5 ←→	5	Ground
Data Set Ready	6 —→	4	Data Terminal Ready
Request to Send	7 —→	8	Clear to Send
Clear to Send	8 ←—	7	Request to Send

Fig. 1.2 An RS-232 Connection Between Two Computers

modem—Fig. 1.2 (shown on the previous page) shows a crossed-connection that is a handy way of directly connecting two computers.

Notice in Fig. 1.2 that pins 2 and 3, pins 4 and 6, and pins 7 and 8 are cross-connected. The Data Set Ready pin, on each side of the interface, sends a continuous signal to the Data Terminal Ready pin, on the other side of the interface, that its computer is on-line and ready to transmit or receive data over the cable. The Request to Send pin sends a signal to the Clear to Send pin when its computer wants to transmit data. The Transmitted Data pin transmits the data—characters—over the cable to the Received Data pin as shown in Fig. 1.1. One method is for one computer to transmit data until it is finished, and at that point stop signalling via the Request to Send pin. The other computer can then use its Request to Send pin to signal the corresponding Clear to Send pin that it is ready to transmit data.

This technique is known as "handshaking" and is the beginning of a protocol. A connection was established and a code was transmitted using an *agreed-upon* set of rules. However, for a data transmission to take the form of a true protocol, messages in the form of PDUs must be transmitted. We will present examples of protocol data units in the next two sections.

1.1.2 The Kermit Protocol

Kermit is a protocol developed in the early 80s at Columbia University for the purpose of transmitting data between computers of different types, such as from personal computers to mainframes. We won't describe the entire Kermit protocol, but only the basics. A Kermit *packet* (PDU) is shown in Fig. 1.3.

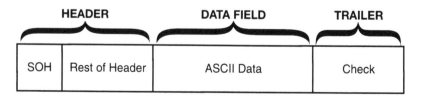

Fig. 1.3 Kermit Packet

As shown in Fig. 1.3, the three main fields of a Kermit packet are: (1) the Header, (2) the Data Field, and (3) the Trailer. Although the contents and function of the detailed formats may vary, the three main fields of nearly all protocol data units—of which the Kermit packet is an example—are the header field, followed by the data field, followed by the trailer field. The header field usually contains control information, and the trailer field usually contains data that can be used for error checking.

A more detailed description of a Kermit packet is shown in Fig. 1.4. MARK, SEQ, and TYPE are subfields of the header field.

MARK	Start of header; usually ASCII SOH.
LEN	Length of packet excluding MARK and CHECK fields; expressed as ASCII decimal digits.
SEQ	Modulo packet sequence number.
TYPE	Type of packet; some of which are:
	D Data Packet
	ACK Acknowledgment Packet (data field empty)
	NAK Negative Acknowledgment Packet (data field empty)
	Z End of File.
DATA	Data Field; contains 0 to 91 characters.
CHECK	Block check on characters in the packet, excluding MARK and CHECK itself. If SUM is the arithmetic sum of the ASCII characters, CHECK = char (SUM + (SUM+ ((SUM AND 192) AND 63))))

Fig. 1.4 Kermit Packet

The AND operator in the CHECK field in Fig. 1.4 is similar to the Boolean AND operator with the difference that every corresponding bit in two bytes is ANDed. Prior to transmission, the computer that is transmitting performs the block check operation indicated in Fig. 1.4, which is then repeated by the computer receiving the packet. If the CHECK fields match, it is assumed the packet was transmitted without error.

Kermit packets whose type field contain either the ACK or NAK ASCII control characters are usually transmitted from the receiver to the sender. An example of how Kermit works is the following:

1. The sender sends a packet with an S in the type field to initialize the transmission.
2. If the receiver transmits an acknowledgment (an ACK in the type field), the sender transmits a packet with an F in the type field to indicate that a file is coming.
3. If the receiver acknowledges by transmitting back an ACK, the sender transmits a data packet.
4. If the receiver acknowledges by transmitting back an ACK, the sender transmits the next data packet.
5. If the receiver transmits a negative acknowledgment (a NAK in the type field) because the block check didn't match the CHECK field, or the sequence number (SEQ field) was incorrect, the sender retransmits the current packet.
6. The sender transmits a packet with Z in the type field, to indicate the end of the file.
7. If the receiver acknowledges by transmitting back an ACK, the sender transmits a packet with a B in the type field to indicate the end of transmission.

Kermit is a *byte* or *character-oriented* protocol that is transmitted in asynchronous mode by using start and stop bits to transmit each character. Transmission of data using Kermit tends to be relatively slow for three reasons:

1. It is a byte-oriented protocol geared for asynchronous transmission (the start and stop bits add to the transmitting overhead).
2. The computer that is transmitting stops after each data packet, waits for an acknowledgment packet from the receiver, processes it, then transmits the next data packet. Kermit was designed for what is called *Half-duplex* transmission.
3. The data field of a Kermit packet is limited to a maximum of 91 bytes, so the header and trailer fields make up a relatively greater portion of each packet, adding to the transmitting and processing overhead.

Most protocols that are used in computer networks are faster and more efficient than Kermit. Kermit is still in use, however, because it is simple and reliable.

1.1.3 HDLC Protocol

High-level Data Link Control (HDLC) is a *bit-oriented* protocol, as opposed to a byte-oriented protocol. HDLC was defined by the International Organization for Standardization to take advantage of technologies that allow synchronous transmission. Synchronous transmission is faster than asynchronous transmission because the sending and receiving clocks are synchronized to allow a prolonged series of bits to be transmitted. With asynchronous transmission the clocks must be re-synchronized by stop and start bits after each character. Many bit-oriented protocols operate similarly to, and conform to, the HDLC protocol.

HDLC has several different modes, including:

1. **Synchronous data link control (SDLC),** which is used in IBM's System Network Architecture (SNA). In fact, IBM did much of the work in the development of HDLC for ISO. SDLC is generally considered a subset of HDLC.

2. The **link-to-link transmission** of an X.25 packet switching network. X.25 is a recommended standard of the ITU-T and is used extensively both in Europe and the U.S. We will describe X.25 in Chapter 4, The Network Layer.

3. **Signalling System 7,** which is the signalling system for the Integrated Services Digital Network (ISDN). ISDN is an ISO standard and will be covered in Chapter 6, High Speed Networks.

4. **Logical Link Control (LLC),** which is used by local area networks (LANs) which are described in Chapter 5, Local Area Networks.

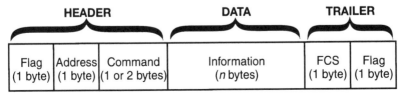

Fig. 1.5 HDLC Frame

An HDLC *frame* is shown in Fig. 1.5 (shown on previous page). The starting and ending delimiters (the *flag* fields in Fig. 1.5) have a unique binary configuration 01111110. When a frame is transmitted, duplication of a flag is avoided by the technique of zero insertion. The transmitter inserts a zero (0) after every five consecutive ones (1), except for the starting and ending flags, and the receiver eliminates every zero (0) that follows five consecutive ones (1).

The address field is used to identify *stations* on the *link*. In computer networks the word "link" means a direct connection with another station, as opposed to a connection that is made over intermediate *nodes* by *routing* or *switching* (we will explain more about routing and switching in Chapter 4, The Network Layer). If two computers are connected by a cable we say they are linked, but no station address is required because each computer has only one other computer to identify. If three or more computers are linked by a cable, transmitted frames may include two address fields, one to identify the transmitting station, and one to identify the receiving station.

A station is any addressable physical or logical "entity" on a link or a network. A computer may be running two or more processes that are addressable logical entities, and thus technically stations. Stations on a link may include highly specialized devices called *bridges* and *routers* that are addressable physical entities, but are not full fledged computers.

HDLC allows both for data and supervisory frames. In a *command frame,* the address field refers to the station that is transmitting. In a *response frame,* the address field refers to the station that is responding. In an information frame, the address field refers to the station that is receiving. In some modes of HDLC there are also special *broadcast frames* that are sent to every station on the link. We will describe the use of the HDLC address and command fields more completely in Chapter 3, The Data-Link Layer.

The size of the information field may vary, with up to *n* bytes allowed. This allows for more efficient data transmission for a frame with a large information field, because the overhead represented by the header and the trailer is relatively small.

The FCS (Frame Check Sequence) field contains what is called a *polynomial* that is used for a type of error checking known as a *cyclic redundancy check* (CRC). We will describe cyclic redundancy checking more completely in Chapter 3.

HDLC was defined as a bit-oriented protocol in order to take advantage of synchronized transmission, but it was also developed to take advantage of technologies that allow *full-duplex* transmission, a type of transmission that allows a device to transmit and receive at the same time. In order to take the maximum advantage of full-duplex transmission, a protocol must allow the transmission of more than one frame without an acknowledgment. In this way when a large file is downloaded from one station to another, both stations can be transmitting and receiving at the same time. The station receiving the downloaded file can be processing information frames and transmitting back acknowledgment frames. The downloading station can be transmitting information frames while simultaneously receiving and processing acknowledgment frames.

The number of PDUs that can be transmitted by the transmitting station before it receives an acknowledgment is called a *window*. HDLC allows windows in two modes: one with a window of up to 7 frames and the other with a window of up to 127 frames.

1.2   Network Topology

Network topologies define the interconnect structure of stations and links. The design issues that are considered in the choice of a network topology are the following:

1. **Expansion cost** - the additional cost of adding new stations to the network.
2. **Reliability** - the resilience of the topology to component failure. Ideally, a network can be easily reconfigured, if a single

station or link fails, so that it can keep working until repairs are made or a faulty component is replaced.

3. **Performance** - in terms of data throughput and the avoidance of delays.

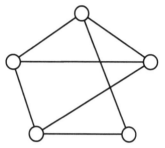

Fig. 1.6 Partial Mesh Topology (partial interconnection)

4. **Network management** - the complexity, and thus the cost, of the software required to manage the network.

Fig. 1.6 shows a *partial mesh* topology, sometimes called a *partial interconnection*. A partial mesh topology has the advantage of high reliability, especially if each station is connected to at least two other stations. In the event of the failure of a link or a station, alternate paths can easily be found.

Partial mesh topologies are used for wide area networks (WANs). There are three kinds of WANs. Public, private, and hybrid (a combination of public and private). Organizations that build private WANs will usually use links that are provided for them by public telephone companies, but will install their own routing equipment and manage

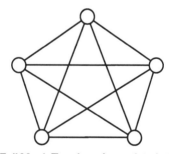

Fig. 1.7 Full Mesh Topology (complete interconnection)

their own network. On the other hand, an organization may simply take advantage of the *public packet switching network* provided by public telephone companies. Or it may build a hybrid of the two.

A type of topology called *full mesh* or *complete interconnection* is shown in Fig. 1.7 (shown on previous page). A complete interconnection provides high throughput because it can operate in parallel and there are no intermediate nodes. If routing is included, this type of topology offers high reliability because it can take advantage of alternate paths between stations.

The number of links required is given by $(n-1)n/2$, where n equals the number of stations, which can result in the installation of a great many expensive communication lines. The complexity of the software

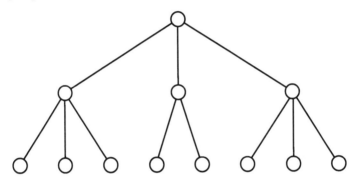

Fig. 1.8 Hierarchical Tree Topology

required to manage this type of network topology can also add to the cost. For these reasons, networks with complete interconnections are seldom used except for highly specialized situations such as military applications, which require extremely high reliability.

Fig. 1.8 shows a *hierarchical tree network*. This type of topology is often used to connect a number of terminals to a central computer that is the root node of the tree. This type of network is similar to the early timesharing system which we discussed in the Introduction. The intermediate nodes consist of various types of communication controllers, such as the concentrator shown in Fig. 1 on page 1.

This type of topology has the disadvantage that a single failure can isolate a part of the network. Also, the trend toward distributed network systems has made hierarchical tree networks less common, though they are still in use. For example, a bank with numerous branches may have terminals used by tellers connected (through concentrators) to a large central computer at the main branch.

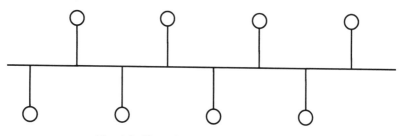

Fig. 1.9 Shared Bus Topology (Highway)

The *shared bus* or *highway* type of network shown in Fig. 1.9 is classified as a broadcast topology. All of the stations are connected by a single transmission line, which minimizes cost. Its biggest advantage is that any PDU that is transmitted can be broadcast to all of the stations. If the PDU is of a type that is meant for all of the stations, then they can all receive it immediately. If it is a type of PDU that is addressed to a single station on the network, it is still received almost immediately.

Another advantage of this type of network topology is that the shared bus can be made completely passive, without moving parts such as relays or even its own power supply, resulting in increased system reliability. It is also easy to add new stations by tapping into the medium, thus reducing expansion costs.

The biggest disadvantage of a shared bus is the possibility of collision if two or more stations try to transmit simultaneously. For this reason, a shared bus is often referred to as a *contention bus*. The software solution for contention bus collision is to have the effected stations attempt to retransmit at random intervals. We will describe contention resolution techniques in more detail in Chapter 5, Local Area Networks. Shared buses are very commonly used for LANs.

Fig. 1.10 shows a *ring* or *loop* topology. When a network is configured in a ring or loop, stations are connected in a unidirectional link. A ring uses a store and forward type of transmission for PDUs, usually called *frames* for this type of network. The frames can be broadcast by letting a frame make a complete circuit of the ring, and then having the station that initiated the transmission remove it. Alternatively, the frame, with only a single destination, can be removed by the destination station.

The advantage of this type of topology is that the problem of con-

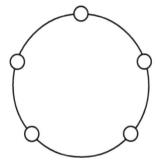

Fig. 1.10 Ring or Loop Topology

tention is easily avoided by using what is called a *token,* which is a type of frame that is continuously passed from station to station when the network is not busy, with only the station in possession of the token being allowed to transmit.

The biggest disadvantage of this type of network topology is that the signal is regenerated at each station, which means the transmission medium cannot be passive. Relays are usually used to bypass stations which have crashed, which add to the complexity of the network. Another method to improve the reliability of a ring network is to use two rings, with one as a backup in case the primary ring fails.

Rings, which are used extensively for local area networks, will be discussed in Chapter 5, Local Area Networks.

Problem Solving Example:

 Two of the most common network topologies are the partial mesh and shared bus. Describe the advantages and disadvantages of each.

Partial Mesh: The principle advantage of a partial mesh is its reliability—if a network node or link fails, alternate paths are available. The principle disadvantage is the complexity of the software needed to manage the network, especially the software used to select routes between network nodes. The partial mesh is commonly used for wide area networks.

Shared bus: The biggest advantage of a shared bus is that it is a broadcast type of topology. Any PDU can be immediately broadcast to any station connected to the bus, with address information used to indicate the source and destination stations. Also, because there is only a single transmission line, cost is minimized. The most significant disadvantage is the possibility of collision if more than one station tries to transmit at the same time. The shared bus is commonly used for local area networks.

1.3   The OSI Reference Model

In the early and mid 1970s separate organizations such as IBM, the defense department's Advanced Research Project Agency, and Digital Equipment were developing their own proprietary network architectures. IBM's proprietary architecture was called System Network Architecture (SNA), the defense department's was called The Advanced Research Project Agency Network (ARPANET), and Digital Equipment's was called Digital Network Architecture (DNA).

What was needed was a broad definition of how heterogeneous systems could interconnect, exchange information, and cooperate in the execution of tasks. In 1977, a subcommittee of the ISO was formed to investigate the need for the standardization of networking functions of computer systems. One of the first tasks of this committee was to define a *Reference Model for Open Systems Interconnection.*

Before we present the work of the ISO subcommittee, we will first examine two concepts of communications: layers and functionality. One of the first network architectures was for the public telephone company. The sequence of events of a telephone call is the following:

1. A station on the public telephone network (a telephone) sends the address (the telephone number) of the station it wants to communicate with to the central office (a system of switches in a mid-sized town).
2. The central office makes a proper connection with the end-station on the network (the telephone being called) with the use of an electronic switch.
3. The central office sends a signal to the end-station (the telephone rings), the end station acknowledges (the telephone is picked up), and there is communication between the two stations (a conversation between the two parties).
4. The conversation is terminated (when both parties say "goodbye").
5. Both parties hang up, causing the switched connection to be released.

The communication in the above example has three layers: (1) the highest layer—the conversation between the two parties, (2) the middle layer—the signalling sent by the telephone to the central office, and by the central office to the other telephone, and (3) the lowest layer—the support provided by the transmission medium, usually a twisted pair of insulated copper wires.

From the standpoint of network architecture, it makes no difference whether the switch in the central office was made manually by a human operator making the connection by inserting a plug with a wire into a socket (as in the early days of telephone networks), or if an electro-mechanical relay was used (which came later), or if the switch was made with a solid-state electronic circuit board (as is the case with modern telephone systems). This is because network architecture is concerned with the *functionality* of a system, not with the underlying technology that implements it.

The ISO subcommittee studied the concept of layers of communication of public telephone networks and proprietary network architectures such as IBM's SNA. Then, in 1980, it presented the OSI Reference Model which defined seven layers of network communication and the functionality of each layer. Systems that conform to the ISO's OSI Reference Model are described as "open."

Fig. 1.11(a) shows the end-to-end communications of the OSI Reference Model. The OSI Reference Model is a layered architecture

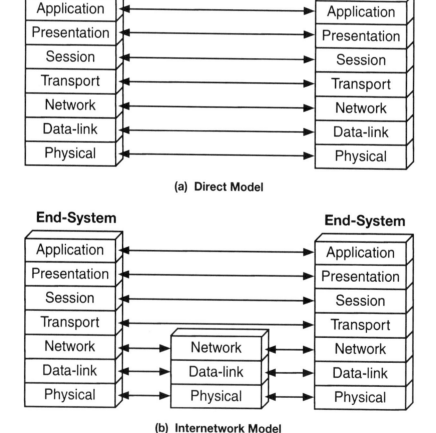

(a) **Direct Model**

(b) **Internetwork Model**

Fig. 1.11 The OSI Reference Model

with the functionality for each layer rigorously defined by a set of documents which is made available by the ISO. Each layer enhances the services of the next lower layer and each layer is a functional unit. Layers 1 and 2 are usually implemented by a combination of hardware and software, while the upper layers can be thought of as software modules. The physical layer consists of the actual physical communications system plus the software drivers for that system.

Fig. 1.11(b) (shown on previous page) shows the extension of the Reference Model for a more complex network that requires the two host systems, or *end-systems,* to communicate through at least one intermediate node. The intermediate nodes are only required to have three layers, with the highest of these three layers being the network layer, which is responsible for routing and switching.

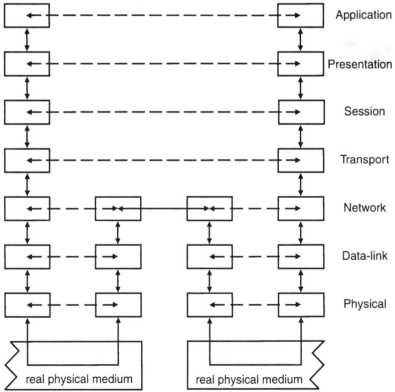

Fig. 1.12 Cooperation Cascade

The arrows in Fig. 1.11 depict the end-to-end communication of "peer entities." Each layer is made up of one or more processes, with each process providing a service within that layer. A process that provides a particular service within a layer is called a *service element* or an entity. If an entity communicates with its peer on another end-system, then we have peer-to-peer communication.

In Fig. 1.12 (shown on previous page), the effective route of peer-to-peer communication is shown by the horizontal, dotted arrows, while the actual route is shown by the vertical arrows. If, for example, an entity in layer n of one end-system sends a message, in the form of a PDU, to its peer entity in layer n of another end-system, the PDU would not be transmitted directly, but would be passed to layer $n-1$ of the transmitting end-system. Then it would be passed to the next lowest layer until it reached the lowest layer, the physical layer, where it would be transmitted as a series of bits to the intermediate node. At the intermediate node the PDU would be passed up each layer to the network layer for routing or switching, then back down, one layer at a time, to the physical layer where it would be transmitted to the receiving end-system. When the PDU reached the receiving end-system it would be passed up, one layer at a time to layer n, where it would be processed by the peer entity of the receiving end-system. Because the peer entities are said to be "cooperating," this process is called a "cooperation cascade."

PDUs are formed by putting together a data field with a header field called the *protocol control information* (PCI). The PDU, as it descends down the stack of layers, is passed to each layer by the use of a mechanism called a *primitive*. Primitives are used to request a service of a lower layer, or by a lower layer to respond to a request that was made by a higher layer. OSI makes no requirements as to how primitives are implemented, but subprogram calls can be used. A primitive can be thought of as a subprogram in one layer calling a subprogram in another layer. A PDU that is passed to another layer can be thought of as one of the parameters of the subprogram.

If a PDU is one of the parameters of a primitive that is "issued" by a higher layer, the PDU parameter is called a *service data unit*

(SDU). Thus, a PDU of layer *n,* of the Reference Model, becomes an SDU in layer *n*–1. The one exception is the highest layer, the application layer, which has passed to it SDUs from the actual application.

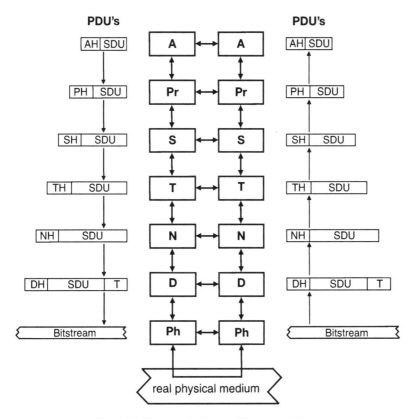

Fig. 1.13 Encapsulation and Decapsulation

As the data to be transmitted cascades down the stack of layers, as shown in Fig. 1.13, each layer adds a header field. The one exception is layer 2, the *data-link layer,* which also adds a trailer field. Some may argue that layer 1, the *physical layer,* does not add a PCI field, but even the physical layer will usually add some kind of synchronization bits in front of the PDU.

As shown in Fig. 1.13, the end-system that receives the PDU strips off the control information as the PDU ascends the stack of layers towards the destination peer entity, until what is left is the original SDU. It should be noted that often all the PCI does, at a particular layer, is tell that layer to pass the PDU up to the next highest layer.

1.4 OSI Reference Model Layers

We will now give a description of the different layers of the OSI Reference Model. The Reference Model itself is elegant in its simplicity. On the other hand, the way the layers actually function is very complex. However, it is important that computer science students get a feel for what is involved in the communication between heterogeneous computers. This lays the conceptual foundation for other computer network topics, which are the mechanics of how things work.

We will describe in more detail the upper four layers. The lower three layers will be covered in greater depth in Chapters 2, 3, and 4 (the physical layer, the data-link layer, and the network layer, respectively).

1.4.1 Layer Seven: The Application Layer

The *application layer* provides system independent services for "application users." Application users are the actual application (a program or package outside the application layer that is usually driven by a human) together with the "application agent."

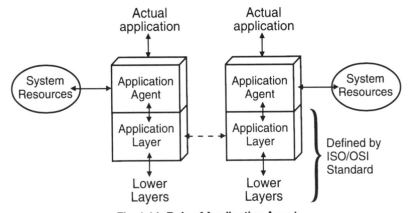

Fig. 1.14 Role of Application Agent

Primitive	Type
A-ASSOCIATE	confirmed
A-RELEASE	confirmed
A-U-ABORT	unconfirmed
A-P-ABORT	provider event, indication only

(a) Control Primitives

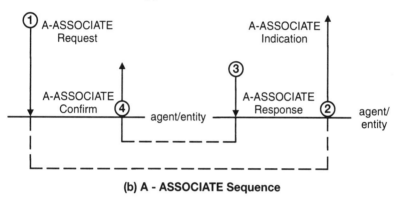

(b) A - ASSOCIATE Sequence

Fig. 1.15 Application Association Control Service Primitives

The application layer interfaces with the actual application and with system resources, such as files stored on a disk, through the application agent. Since the application agent is clearly system dependent, it is not part of the ISO/OSI Model. Fig. 1.14 (on previous page) shows how application entities interface with the application user and system resources.

An application agent establishes an "association" between cooperating application entities by issuing what is called the A- ASSOCIATE primitive, which contains an SDU and other parameters for the presentation layer. Fig. 1.15(a) shows the association control primitives and Fig. 1.15(b) shows the association establishment process. The indication, response, and confirm shown in Fig. 1.15(b) are also primitives which also contain parameters and possibly SDUs. Primitives that only result in an indication and not in a response and confirm are called "unconfirmed" (see Fig. 1.15(a)).

In addition to application control primitives, there are primitives issued for specific application services such as file transfer, electronic messaging (e-mail), job transfer, and virtual terminal which are ISO/OSI standards. An application layer may contain many application entities, each providing a specific service, and with each service request made by issuing a specific primitive.

The "user" of the application layer is the actual application, usually driven by a human, together with the application agent, as explained earlier. The user of all other layers is the next highest layer. Each layer provides services for its user, when requested.

1.4.2   Layer Six: The Presentation Layer

The *presentation layer* is responsible for "representing" data that is transmitted from a remote end-system in such a way that it is comprehensible to the application layer. For example, integers in one computer may be represented by 32 bits and in another by 16 bits. It is the presentation layer's responsibility to convert the data portion of a PDU to the representation understood by the receiving end-system before passing the PDU to the application layer in the form of an SDU.

Another example is EBCDIC character representation on one end-system converted by the presentation layer to ASCII character representation on another end-system. Other possible examples include the representation of floating point and negative numbers.

The structure of data that is stored in files on a disk has nothing to do with the presentation layer and is left up to system software outside the Reference Model. However, the structure of memory resident data such as records is a concern of the presentation layer. For example, a record with three fields—an integer, a Boolean, and sequence of characters—could be represented differently on two different end-systems.

The unit of information contained in a PDU formed by the presentation layer is called the information unit, which makes up the data portion of the PDU. The precise definition of the data contained in an information unit that is independent of system representation is called the *abstract syntax*. The abstract syntax is usually included in the PCI part of the PDU, which allows the remote end-system to make the appropriate transformation of the data which it receives.

Another possibility is that cooperating peer presentation entities may agree that the transformation of the data will take place before the information unit is transmitted. In this case, both end-systems need to know the other's representation of each abstract syntax.

The application user on the initiating end-system may also request that the data, that is transmitted back and forth, be encrypted, or that redundant sequences be compressed. How the data is converted, prior to transmission, is called the transfer syntax. The transfer syntax may include any combination of three successive stages:

1. The **transformation** of data to the way it is represented on the destination end-system.
2. **Compression** of redundant sequences.
3. **Encryption.**

The transfer syntax may, in some cases, include none of these three stages. In other words, the data may be simply be transmitted the way it is.

The application layer requests the establishment of a presentation layer "connection" between two end-systems with the P-CONNECT primitive. The P-CONNECT primitive includes several parameters, one of which is the context definition list (the set of abstract syntaxes which will be required). The presentation entity, which negotiates the connection, transmits a PDU that contains the required abstract syntaxes, with each one paired with a group of possible choices of a transfer syntax. The peer entity on the remote end-system responds with its choice of a transfer syntax for each abstract syntax, if it can find one that is acceptable. If the peer entity cannot find at least one transfer syntax that is acceptable for each abstract syntax, then the negotiation fails, and the presentation connection is not established. If the negotiation succeeds, the pairing of a transfer syntax with each abstract syntax is called the defined context set (DCS).

The presentation layer also provides a "mirroring service" between the application and *session layers*. An example is when the P-CONNECT primitive is issued by the application layer. Most of the P-CONNECT parameters are simply passed on the session layer by the issuing of a S-CONNECT request. Also, the parameters of the S-CONNECT indication, which indicates a session connection has been made, are also passed on to the application layer as parameters of a P-CONNECT indication. Fig. 1.16 shows the S-CONNECT service primitive sequence.

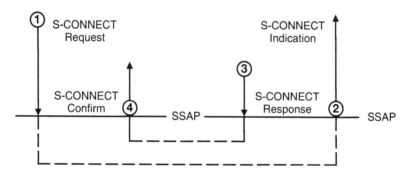

Fig. 1.16 S-CONNECT Service Primitive Sequence

Layers communicate with each other through *service access points* (SAPs). The SSAP in Fig. 1.16 stands for "session service access point." The presentation layer is said to have established a connection once the DCS has been negotiated and the session connection has been established. However, this is not a true end-to-end data communications connection. The maintenance of the data communications connection or "channel" between end-systems is the responsibility of the session layer.

1.4.3   Layer Five: The Session Layer

The establishment and maintenance of sessions between end-systems is the responsibility of the session layer. Data transmitted through the session layer is "transparent;" by this we mean only the higher layers are concerned with the contents of the information units that are transmitted between end-systems. The session layer provides a channel through which a series of "octets" is transparently transmitted and received.

One of the services provided by the session layer is the addressing of higher layers. If we think of the presentation layer as providing a mirroring service between the session layer and the application layer, then those two layers can be considered one layer: the session service user. Fig. 1.17 shows the addressing of the higher layers provided by the session layer, through the session service access point (SSAP).

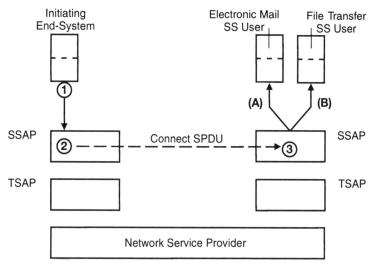

Fig. 1.17 Addressing of A & B SS User

One of the most important services provided by the session layer is the insertion of synchronization points between service data units. The issuance of the synchronization points is the responsibility of the application layer, but the insertion and identity (the serial number) is the responsibility of the session layer.

There are two types of synchronization points: "major" and "minor." A major synchronization point indicates the end of one dialogue unit and the start of the next. The minor synchronization points are to indicate commonly understood points of reference within a dialogue unit.

The synchronization points are used to resynchronize from a point where data is known to be secured or to restart activities. The user of

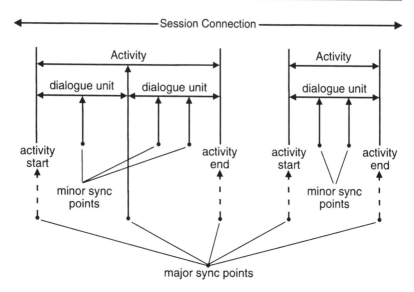

Fig. 1.18 Synchronization of Activities

the application service layer may start, restart, or abandon several activities during a session as shown in Fig. 1.18.

The session layer uses the synchronization points, together with what is called the activity service element, to maintain a session. Peer application entities are said to be associated rather than connected because there may be several associations established and released while the session layer maintains the connection.

1.4.4 Layer Four: The Transport Layer

The *transport layer* is responsible for transparent data transfer between two session entities. The transport layer is responsible for end-to-end flow control and it enhances the underlying network by providing a guaranteed quality of service.

The underlying network is responsible for error detection and correction; however, there are two types of network errors that the transport layer must take into account in order to provide the quality of service provided by the higher layers:

1. **Signalled errors,** such as network reset or network disconnection.
2. **Residual errors** not detected by the network layer.

If there is more than one sub-network between two end-stations (one example would be a partial mesh WAN interconnected by a router to a shared bus LAN), then the transport layer must be aware of the rate of both signalled and residual errors of each of the subnetworks.

The *quality of service* (QOS) requested by the session layer depends on the following factors:

1. **Reliability** - the rate of disconnects.
2. **Resilience** - the time required to recover from a disconnect, and the rate of successful recovery.
3. **Throughput** - octets transmitted per unit time.
4. **Accuracy** - residual error rate of the data presented by the transport layer to the session layer.

The QOS is negotiated by peer session entities when a session connection is established. If, for example, the throughput that can be provided by the transport layer is too low, the session layer negotiation may fail and it may issue a T-DISCONNECT primitive.

In order to provide the added throughput, the transport layer may "split" the transmission onto two network connections. Splitting requires that the peer transport entity on the remote end-system keep track of the order of TPDUs, so that the data units are kept in their proper sequence.

The transport layer provides end-to-end flow control in the following way:

1. When the transport connection is made, the transport layers on both end-systems negotiate a "window." The window is the number of TPDUs that each transport layer can transmit before an acknowledgment is received from the other end-

system. The size of the window is basically equal to the number of buffers available for temporary storage of TPDUs on the other end-system.

2. The transmitting transport layer decrements the window counter each time it transmits a TPDU.

3. The transmitting transport layer increments the window counter each time it receives an acknowledgment from the transport layer on the receiving end-system.

4. If the window counter is equal to zero, the transport layer discontinues transmission until at least one acknowledgment is received.

Another service that the transport layer must provide, if requested by the higher layers, is expedited data. The transport layer's expedited data mechanism will work in conjunction with the network layer's, if there is one. If it is not available for that network, then the expedited effect is provided entirely within the transport layer.

The expedited data effect is related to flow control. If the window is closed because the window counter is zero, then the transport layer accumulates TPDUs in a buffer as a result of the session layer continuing to issue T-DATA primitives. The TPDUs in this buffer are "queued" on a first in-first out basis.

When the window opens (because of the reception of an acknowledgment), if there are any ED TPDUs (expedited data TDPUs) in the queue, as a result of a T-EXPEDITED-DATA request from the session layer, they are moved to the front of the queue and transmitted. As the number of queued TPDUs decrease, because data transmission has resumed, ED TPDUs will continue to be moved to the front of the queue until the size of the queue is zero. Fig. 1.19 (on next page) depicts the expedited data service mechanism.

As shown in Fig. 1.19, when the AK TPDU (acknowledgment TPDU) is received by the transmitting transport layer, event 7, the window opens and the ED TPDU is transmitted from the front of the queue.

1.4.5   Layer Three: The Network Layer

The network layer is responsible for routing and switching of packets across a complex network which includes intermediate nodes. The network layer may provide what is called a *virtual circuit* or a *virtual path* between end-systems—usually referred to as switching—or it may provide the dynamic selection of alternate routes to by-pass congested links and to maintain a smooth flow of data traffic—usually referred to as routing. We will provide a more in-depth discussion of the network layer in Chapter 4.

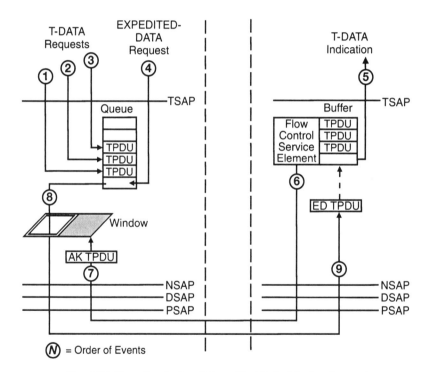

Fig. 1.19 Flow Control and Expedited Data Mechanisms of Transport Layer

1.4.6   Layer Two: The Data-link Layer

The data-link layer provides transmission across a direct link. The direct link may be between two end-systems, or in the case of a more complex network, the direct link is either between an end-system and an intermediate node, or between two intermediate nodes. The data-link layer is responsible for link level error detection and correction and also for link level flow control. We will describe the data-link layer in greater detail in Chapter 3.

1.4.7 Layer One: The Physical Layer

The physical layer defines the interface to the real physical medium for the transmission of data. This layer specifies the electrical and mechanical protocols for the transfer of bits between two devices on a network. It includes the communications hardware and the software drivers. The physical layer is the subject of Chapter 2.

1.5 Client-Server Architecture

The *client-server model* is a distributed type of architecture that allows PCs and workstations to perform tasks previously performed in a mainframe communications environment. In a client-server environment, a client process on one computer will usually provide a graphical interface which allows the user to interface with a server process on another computer to perform such tasks as:

1. **Remote access** to files.
2. **Remote printing.**
3. **Shared applications** where files and even application functions are shared between the client and the server.
4. **Transactions** with a remote database.

Servers allow multiple threads of code to execute concurrently, thus multiple clients may be served at the same time.

1.5.1 Socket Interface

The *socket application programming interface* (API) was originally developed for use with the Berkeley Software Distribution (BSD) version of the UNIX operating system. The socket API can be used: (1) to set up interfaces within the same host, allowing separate UNIX processes to communicate, (2) to communicate using OSI protocols, or (3) for communication with Xerox's XNS protocols. The socket is also the most widely used interface with the Internet's protocol suite, TCP/IP.

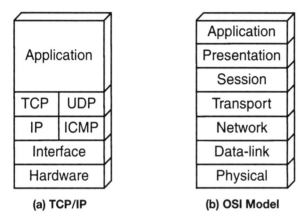

(a) TCP/IP   (b) OSI Model

Fig. 1.20 Comparison of Layered Architectures of TCP/IP and OSI

1.5.2   Transport Control Protocol/Internet Protocol (TCP/IP)

The TCP/IP protocol suite is used on the worldwide Internet and also for internetworking on many independent networks. A comparison of the OSI Reference Model and TCP/IP is shown in Fig. 1.20.

The application layer of TCP/IP is roughly equivalent to the upper three layers of OSI. There is no real equivalent of a presentation layer, so it is the application program's responsibility to ensure that data is represented in a way that is comprehensible to both systems. For example, many computers such as Intel-based PCs represent integers in a big-endian format, with bytes stored in reverse order of significance. TCP/IP assumes big-endian as a default, but also makes available function calls that will cause little-endian to be converted to big-endian. Also, client-server applications employ a wide range of methods for data description, including using the international standard abstract syntax notation one (ASN.1), described in Section 7.7 of Chapter 7.

There is no session layer, but the establishment of a remote connection is still costly, and it is an important design issue of client-server software to be able to perform as many tasks as possible before a connection is relinquished.

The OSI committee took a good look at TCP, which was being used on the ARPANET, when they wrote the specifications for the OSI transport layer. The capabilities of the two transport protocols are actually quite similar. One important difference is that there is no provision for TCP to negotiate a network connection based on minimal requirements and maximal desires of throughput and reliability. Another important difference is that, although TCP provides for an urgent data capability, it is different from the OSI's expedited TPDUs in that an embedded escape character will cause a specified number of octets to be processed first, by the receiver.

The User Datagram Protocol (UDP), which can be used as an option to TCP, provides for an unreliable, connectionless delivery of UDP protocol data units. In other words, no connection is negotiated, established, or maintained. It is up to the end-system application processes to establish and maintain an association, and to insure the integrity of data.

IP is a connectionless protocol that provides network layer services. IP is responsible for routing protocol data units, called *datagrams,* across an interconnected network. If TCP is selected as the transport protocol, then, when IP datagrams are passed up to the transport layer, out of sequence PDUs are reordered and if one is lost, retransmission is requested. The concept of a connectionless datagram type of delivery is important, and will be developed further in subsequent chapters.

The network interface is sometimes described as the TCP/IP equivalent to the data-link layer. It is responsible for interfacing with the type of network the IP datagram is being routed across. Often this results in the IP datagram being encapsulated in a data-link layer PDU before being transmitted across a point-to-point link. At other times the network interface is required to interface with a more complex network that has its own network layer protocol—with the network interface causing the IP datagram to eventually arrive at an IP node at the other end of the network.

1.5.3 Socket Addresses

When the TCP/IP protocol suite is used, the *socket address* contains the following three values:

1. **Protocol Family** - a 16-bit integer identifying the protocol family—in this case TCP/IP.
2. **Port Number** - a 16-bit integer which identifies the port number assigned to the process. The client must know the port number of the client process. The client usually identifies itself with an "ephemeral" port number, which it requests from the communications software.
3. **IP Address** - an IP address is a 32-bit number used to logically identify a device on an IP network.

Fig. 1.21 shows the three types of sockets. The stream socket is used when TCP is the transport protocol because the service provided

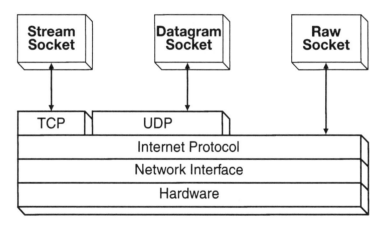

Fig. 1.21 Types of Sockets

is a reliable, in-sequence stream of octets. The datagram socket is used when UDP is selected because the service provided is an unreliable transport of datagrams. The "raw" socket is used when the application interfaces directly with IP. The type of socket is represented by an integer.

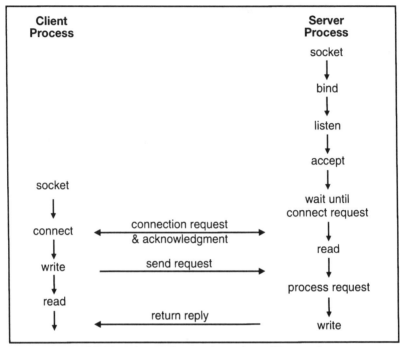

(a) Client Server Connection-oriented Protocol

```
socket  (
         Internet-Family,
         Sock-Stream,
         0
       );
```

(b) Socket System Call

Fig. 1.22 System Calls

1.5.4   System Calls

A set of system calls is provided by the socket API. These *system calls* are invoked by application programs to request communication services. Since the UNIX operating system was written in C language, often the code for system calls is in C, but they can be written in any language. If C is used on a UNIX system, the following include statements will make data structures available that can be used for system calls:

1. include <sys/type.h>
2. include <sys/sockets.h>

Fig. 1.22(a) (shown on previous page) depicts the sequence of system calls necessary to establish a TCP connection between a client and a server. Fig. 1.22(b) shows the code segment for the socket system call. *Internet-Family* and *Socket-Stream* are defined constants which identify the protocol family and type of socket, respectively. Other system calls may require, as parameters, pointers to the socket address of either the client or server. Socket addresses are represented in C by structures with three integer fields: the family, the port, and the IP address. Table 1.3 describes the other system calls shown in Fig. 1.22(a).

System calls may not seem to be part of a layered architecture, but they can be thought of as the equivalent of the application agent of the OSI Model. Like the application agent, they are system-dependent and provide an interface between the protocol "stack," the communications application, and system resources.

Socket	Initializes a socket data structure, identifies the transport layer protocol, and obtains integer descriptor of socket.
Bind	Associates an internet address and port number with the integer descriptor of the open socket.
Listen	Indicates that server process is ready to accept a request from a client—used by TCP application processes.
Accept	Causes server to wait for connection request from client—used by application processes employing TCP.
Connect	Establishes a TCP connection with server.
Read	Used to accept incoming data from socket.
Write	Used to send data over a socket.

Table 1.3 Socket System Calls

Problem Solving Examples:

 What is meant by a layered architecture? Contrast and compare the layered architectures of the OSI Reference Model and TCP/IP.

 A layered network architecture is a type of architecture where each layer provides a service for the next higher layer and each layer enhances the service provided by the next lower layer. Also, each layer utilizes one or more protocols to communicate with its peer, over a direct link, or across a complex network.

The OSI Reference Model is meant to provide a detailed model for an open systems interconnection, rather than an architecture that is actually implemented. TCP/IP is actually implemented, but its purpose is the interconnection of different physical networks, which may not operate with the same data-link protocols.

Apart from being defined for different purposes, TCP/IP does not have the equivalent of OSI's session or presentation layers, so those functions are performed by the application layer.

 What is meant by a distributed network? Why is the client-server model considered a form of distributed networking? Draw a simple diagram of a client-server architecture—assume the TCP/IP protocol suite is used for network communication.

 A network is considered distributed if data, processing power, and control are distributed throughout the network.

The client-server model allows PCs and workstations to perform tasks that were once performed by larger, more powerful, mainframe computers. The application components are divided between the "client" and the "server." Thus, the distributed application components, including files, and even processes, are an integral part of the client-server model.

Fig. 1.23 Client-server architecture for TCP/IP internetworking

Fig. 1.23 shows a client-server architecture assuming the use of TCP/IP for internetworking.

1.6 Definition of Network Architecture

Here is a comprehensive definition of network architecture:

A computer network is a distributed system of autonomous computers, in which each computer can exchange data with any other computer in the system. By data we mean a sequence of binary digits that has meaning in at least two places in the network, these being the source and destination of that data. An abstract definition of events that initiate data exchange, the mechanisms involved in setting up such exchanges, and how these are managed define a network architecture. A network architecture refers to the functional view of the system as opposed to the technology used to implement it.

CHAPTER 2

The Physical Layer

The physical layer is extremely important as the extraordinary advances in this area that will allow the information superhighways of the next century to be built. These technological advances include: (1) transmitting to residences at rates of up to 6 mbps over existing telephone lines, (2) transmission speeds over optical fiber trunk lines at rates exceeding one trillion bits per second.

Fig. 2.1 shows the basic structure of the physical layer of a computer network that applies both for LANs and for WANs utilizing the public telephone network.

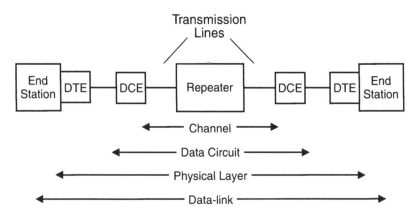

Fig. 2.1 Data Transmission Components

2.1 Functions of Transmission Components

The transmission components shown in Fig. 2.1 perform functions discussed below.

2.1.1 Transmission Line

This could be a *twisted pair* of insulated copper wires, a *fiber optic* cable, or a *coaxial cable* (a cable with a conducting shell and a conducting inner core with the same "axis"). All three of these type of cables are used in networks that range from local area networks of a few hundred feet to wide area networks thousands of miles across.

Although still in the minority, the use of optical fiber in LANs has been around for ten years. As computers become more powerful and able to support applications that involve the transfer of huge amounts of data, such as imaging applications, *optical fiber* will comprise the "physical support" for a significant portion of local area networks.

The cables that provide data transmission for metropolitan area networks (MANs) and WANs are usually accessed by means of the public telephone service. Thus, Fig. 2.1 can be said to apply to MANs and WANs with the transmission lines being supplied by the public telephone network. The cables used by telephone companies are also twisted pairs, coaxial cable, and optical fiber, although coaxial cable is becoming increasingly rare. In some cases an organization will install its own wide area cable links.

Also, the transmission line in Fig. 2.1 could be considered a radio wave link between a satellite and a "ground station" or a "microwave" link between two "towers." The best way to think of the transmission line in Fig. 2.1 is as a *passive medium* which is used to propagate a signal between two points.

Cables are often depicted, in computer science literature (particularly in figures), as the real physical medium, as the physical support, or as the passive medium. Because cables are important, they will be covered in Sections 2.6 and 2.7. However, the reader should be aware that it is by the broader definition of the physical layer that cables are included in this chapter.

2.1.2 Regenerative Repeater

The repeater regenerates either an analog or digital signal that has begun to weaken or become distorted. Fig. 2.2 shows a regenerated binary signal.

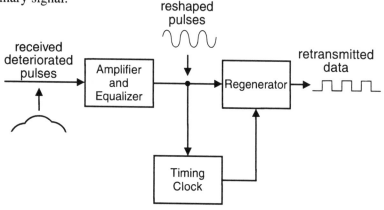

Fig. 2.2 Block Diagram of Regenerative Repeater

Repeaters are part of the "channel" (see Fig. 2.1). A regenerative repeater is not passive media. It includes electrical and mechanical devices that actually have a measurable impact on the transmitted signal and a repeater is thus considered part of the physical layer—even by the strict definition of physical layer. From a logical or functional view, however, all a repeater does is repeat the signal, and, in this sense, can be viewed as part of the transmission line.

Repeaters are also used in a wide range of networks from LANs to WANs, and also are often used as part of the public telephone service.

2.1.3 Channel

By channel we mean a data channel. More than one data channel can be multiplexed onto a single transmission line. More about multiplexers and similar devices in will be explained in Section 2.4.

2.1.4 Data Circuit Terminating Equipment (DCE)

These are also known as data communications equipment. The most common type of DCE equipment is the modem. A modem, or modulator/demodulator converts (modulates) the digital signal it receives from the DTE device (see Fig. 2.1) to an analog signal that can be transmitted over the public telephone network. This analog signal must be understood by the receiving DCE device at the other end of the data circuit (see Fig. 2.1) so it can be decoded (demodulated).

There are two important things to remember about DCE equipment:

1. The digital signal received from the DTE by a DCE device is already in serial form (this is a function of DTE equipment). A good example of serial data transmission is the asynchronous transmission of ASCII characters (see Fig. 1.1 on page 8).
2. DCEs are not necessarily modems. The data transmission of a DCE is not necessarily in analog form; some DCEs transmit data in digital form. An example is the digital service unit/channel service unit (DSU/CSU), which is used to take advantage of the Dataphone Digital Service (DDS) offered almost universally by local public telephone services. DDS allows digital data to be transmitted at data rates of 56-64 kilobits per second with the DSU/CSU acting almost as a digital modem.

A DCE device accepts digital data in serial form, from a DTE device, and transforms that data to a signal (analog *or* digital) that is acceptable to the channel and that can also be decoded by the DCE on the other end. The receiving DCE decodes the data and in turn transfers it in digital serial form to its own DTE.

It is tempting to think of serially transmitted digital data as just a series of zeros and ones; however, there are many different ways to encode digital data on a transmission line. Section 2.5 examines some of the more important encoding techniques.

2.1.5 Data Terminal Equipment (DTE)

Data is accessed and stored internally by a computer in parallel. That is, if a computer has a 16-bit word, it will write or read every one of those 16 bits simultaneously. It is the function of "data terminal equipment" to convert parallel data to a serial format. To give a technical definition, a DTE device terminates the data transmission by accepting serial data from a DCE device and by converting that data to parallel so that it can be used by a host computer or end-station, or by accepting data in parallel from an end-station and outputting that data serially to a DCE device. DTE equipment is also responsible for insertion of parity bits and for parity error-checking.

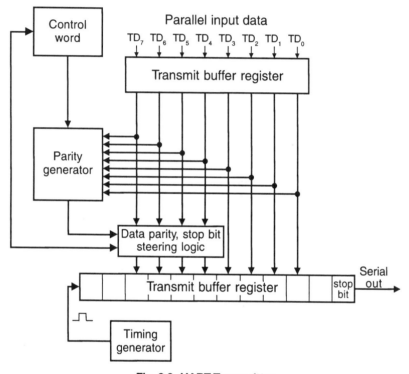

Fig. 2.3 UART Transmitter

Fig. 2.3 shows the block diagram of the transmitter of one of the most common components of DTE devices—a universal asynchronous receiver/transmitter (UART). As shown in Fig. 2.3, the data is received in parallel and output serially complete with start, stop, and parity bits (all three of which are generated logically and depend on the control word of the UART). The diagram of the receiver of a UART is similar, except it does the same thing in reverse—with the receiver being responsible for parity error checking. Another common component of DTE devices is the universal synchronous receiver/transmitter (USRT), which transmits a SYN character to the DCE prior to transmission (see

Table 1.2). Since the USRT is synchronous there is clocking information transferred between it and the DCE.

An example of DTE equipment is the serial port of a PC. A serial port card with a UART or a USRT or both can be plugged into the expansion slot of a PC. The serial port card allows devices from the outside world, such as external modems, to be connected to the computer. A "front-end processor" is also a type of DTE. A front-end processor accepts serial data from several sources and transfers the data in parallel to a large computer. Front-end processors include software capability.

The term data terminal equipment has come to mean a terminal or PC that is an end-station on a network, or in the case of a large computer the term DTE may refer to a front-end processor that is a separate stand-alone device.

The reason we gave a detailed explanation of the strict definition of data terminal equipment and its function is that one of the most important sets of standards in the data communications world are "serial interface standards," which interface DTE and DCE equipment. It is important to know how the term DTE developed even though in practice the term often refers to a terminal or PC. We will cover "serial interfaces" in Section 2.2.

2.1.6 Physical Layer

The physical layer includes the physical communications equipment and only those software modules that drive the DTE and DCE equipment. The physical layer may be responsible for limited error-checking such as parity checking. It receives data from the data-link layer in a series of bits, or perhaps in a series of bytes, but the information contained in those bits or bytes are transparent to the physical layer.

2.2 Serial Interface Standards

Before serial interfaces were standardized, every company that manufactured communications equipment used a different interface configuration. To interconnect computers and communication equipment from different vendors required building level converters and special cables and connectors. The Telecommunications Industries Association/Electronic Industries Association (TIA/EIA), in order to facilitate computer communication, agreed on the TIA/EIA-232 serial interface. This standard has been updated several times, the last time in 1998, which resulted in the TIA/EIA-232-F.

An TIA/EIA standard is properly referred to by TIA/EIA-(standard number). However, TIA/EIA standards have been popularly referred to by RS-(standard number), with RS standing for "recommended standard." Thus, the TIA/EIA-232 became almost universally known as the RS-232.

Although the RS-232 interface is simply a cable and two connectors, the standard specifies limitations on the voltage levels the DTE and DCE can output. Also, since this is a digital interface, the voltage levels of the pins represent either a logic 0 or a logic 1. In both DCE and DTE equipment there are circuits called "levelers" that convert the internal logic levels to RS-232 values. A leveler is called a "driver" if it outputs a voltage signal and a "terminator" if it accepts a voltage signal. Fig. 2.4 (on next page) shows the voltage levels, their limitations, and logical equivalents for the RS-232 interface.

| | Data Pins | |
	Logic 1	Logic 0
Driver	-5 to -15	+5 to +15
Terminator	-3 to -25	+3 to +25
	Control Pins	
	Enable "on"	Disable "off"
Driver	+5 to +15	-5 to -15
Terminator	+3 to +25	-3 to -25

Table 2.1 RS-232 Voltage Specifications

As shown in Table 2.1, the limits for a driver are more inclusive than those for a terminator. The difference in the voltage levels between the driver and the terminator is called the "noise margin."

There are two types of RS-232 connectors that are used: a 9-pin connector called a DB-9 and a 25-pin connector called a DB-25.

Fig. 2.4(a) shows the configuration of the DB-9 connector and Fig. 2.4(b) the configuration of the DB-25 connector. The DB-25 has the same overall configuration except the top row of the male connector is numbered 1 through 13 and the bottom row is numbered 14 through 25.

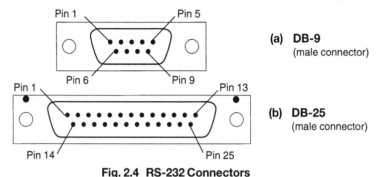

Fig. 2.4 RS-232 Connectors

The cables used with RS-232 connectors consist of 25 parallel insulated copper wires inside a larger casing with a thickness of about 3/8". The standard defines an exact circuit function for each of the 25 pins, although they may not all be used. Obviously not all of the pin functions are used with the 9-pin version. Although we won't describe the circuit function for every pin, Table 2.2 describes the circuit functions for some of the pins that are used in almost every application. The

	Pin Number	Direction	Description
(a) Control Pins	4	DTE to DCE	RTS, Request to Send. The computer signals the modem that it is ready to send data.
	5	DCE to DTE	CTS, Clear to Send. The modem signals the computer it is ready to accept data.
	6	DCE to DTE	DSR, Data Set Ready. The modem signals the computer that it is connected to the telephone line.
	8	DCE to DTE	DCD, Data Carrier Detect. The modem tells the computer that it has gone on line and the computer can receive data.
	20	DTE to DCE	DTR, Data Terminal Ready. The computer signals the modem that it is powered up.
(b) Data Pins	2	DTE to DCE	TD, Transmitted Data. The computer transmits data to the modem on this pin.
	3	DCE to DTE	RD, Received Data. The computer receives data on this pin.

Table 2.2 RS-232 Pin Designations

pins described in Table 2.2(a) are used for handshaking and control and the pins described in Table 2.2(b) are used for data transmission.

Pins 2 and 3 allow for a "full duplex" data channel—the simultaneous transmission and reception of data. Some of the pin functions not shown in Table 2.2 allow for a secondary full duplex channel that may used for special purposes such as diagnostics. Some other pin functions include synchronization and clocking signals that allow DTE equipment with USRTs to interface DCE equipment.

An additional electrical characteristic that was specified by the TIA/EIA for the RS-232 standard was the terminal load capacitance of 2500 pico Farads for a cable length of typically 50 ft. Although a discussion of capacitance is beyond the scope of this book, in general the greater the capacitance the slower the digital data rate. A capacitance of 2500 pico Farads allows a data transfer rate of 20 kilobits per second between DTE and DCE equipment, which was very fast at the time. The following are examples of RS-232 applications far exceeding the specified maximum data rate:

1. Today's modems commonly transmit and receive data at rates of 33.6 kbps (see Unit Abbreviations at the back of this book). Since these modems are also capable of data compression, the transfer rate between a PC (DTE equipment) and an external modem (DCE equipment) can be as high as 115 kbps.

2. CSU/DSUs (DCE equipment) which are commonly connected to computers or front-end processors (DTE equipment) by a RS-232 interface, transmit and receive digital data at rates of 56-64 kbps using DDS, offered by the public telephone service.

3. Another digital transmission service offered by most public telephone companies is the Integrated Services Digital Network (covered in Chapter 6). The data transfer rate between what is called an ISDN modem (DCE equipment) and a computer (DTE equipment) using a RS-232 interface can be as high as 128 kbps.

This sounds like the RS-232-E standard is routinely disregarded, but that is not really true. What has happened is that each new revision must be backwards compatible, so that the original maximum data rate of 20 kbps has never been increased. However, manufacturers have continued to adhere to the terminal load capacitance of 2500 pico Farads, but with cable lengths of around 200 ft. versus the original of 50 ft. Thus, a 50 ft. cable has a capacitance of much less than 2500 pico Farads. The result is that an RS-232-E interface with a cable length of only a few feet, or even 50 ft. can easily handle the data rates described.

Fig. 1.2 in Section 1.1.1 (page 9) showed a possible arrangement for using an RS-232 cable to connect two computers. Fig. 2.5 shows the pin numbers and nomenclature of a possible arrangement for connecting a DTE device to a DCE device using DB-9 connectors. In contrast to Fig. 1.2, there are no cross-connections in Fig. 2.5, because a computer (DTE equipment) is connected to a modem (DCE equipment). In effect, the cross-connected arrangement shown in Fig. 1.2 fooled the computers into behaving as though they were communicating through modems, when they were really directly connected to each other.

DB - 9 (DCE) Function	Pin No.	Pin No.	DB - 9 (DTE) Function
Frame Ground	1 ←→	1	Frame Ground
Transmitted Data	2 ←	2	Transmitted Data
Received Data	3 →	3	Received Data
Request to Send	4 ←	4	Request to Send
Clear to Send	5 →	5	Clear to Send
Data Set Ready	6 →	6	Data Set Ready
Signal Ground	7 ←→	7	Signal Ground
Data Carrier Detect	8 →	8	Data Carrier Detect
Not Used	9 —	9	Not Used

Fig. 2.5 An RS-232 Connection Between a DCE Device and a DTE Device

Fig. 2.6 (on next page) shows a possible real-world application that would require standardized serial interface equipment with cable lengths in excess of a few feet. As shown in Fig. 2.6, a number of computers with modems on a wide area network are connected to a central site by utilizing a public telephone network service called a T1 line (we will describe T1 lines in more detail in Section 2.7). Since a T1 line has 24 channels, in Fig. 2.6 there would be 24 DCE devices (modems, DSU/CSUs, ISDN modems, etc.) connected by 24 RS-232 cables to DTE equipment (PCs, terminals, front-end processors, etc.). If there were several incoming T1 lines there could be hundreds of RS-232 cables connected to various "campus" locations.

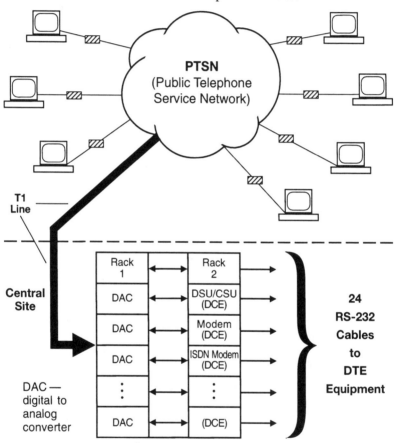

Fig. 2.6 Application for RS-232 Interface

Some of these lines would be bound to have cable lengths (in excess of 200 ft.) that would result in an increase in terminal load capacitance beyond the standard's allowable 2500 pico Farads. In other words, the cable length would only allow prohibitively slow data rates (much less than 20 kbps). Section 2.2.1 briefly discusses other serial interfaces that allow greater data rates and longer cables.

2.2.1 Other Serial Interface Standards

The RS-449 was developed as an eventual replacement for the RS-232. The RS-449 is a mechanical standard supported by the RS-422-A, which is an electrical standard. When the RS-449, which comes in a 9-pin and 37-pin configuration, is operating with the RS-422-A electrical standard, it is capable of data rates of 2 megabits per second with a maximum cable length of 200 ft. The RS-422-A achieves this data rate by modulating the transmitted signal with an inverse copy of the same signal on another wire, thus allowing greater immunity to noise. The EI TIA/E530, which uses a 25-pin connector, has also been growing in popularity. The advantage of the TIA/EIA-530 is that it allows digital connections of up to 500 ft.

2.3 Modems

Serial digital data is transmitted from DTE equipment to DCE equipment by varying the voltage level of a direct current circuit. For example, if an RS-232 interface is used, a voltage level between −15 V and −5 V is a logic 1 and a voltage level between +5 V and +15 V is a logic 0. However, telephone lines operate with alternating current and use analog electronics. Analog electronics represent signals with smoothly flowing changes in current or voltage while digital electronics are characterized by rapid transitions to discrete voltage levels, which are then held for a short, but specified time interval (see Fig. 1.1 on page 8).

In order to transmit digital data over an analog phone line, a modem is required. A modem works by first introducing a carrier onto the transmission line: a continuous sine wave with a frequency of about 2000 hz. The high-pitched tone that a caller may hear when accidentally dialing a fax machine is an example of a carrier.

The carrier is "modulated" by the modem in such a way that the digital signal is encoded into the outgoing analog signal. The modem performs this encoding by changing (modulating) one to three aspects of the carrier signal: (1) the frequency (the pitch of the tone is varied), (2) the amplitude (the loudness is varied), or (3) the phase (phase modulation is described in Section 2.2.2). The modem at the other end of the transmission line decodes ("demodulates") the analog signal, outputting the corresponding digital signal that is fed serially into DTE equipment.

Before we explain how modems work, we will first take a look at maximum possible data rates, because today's modems are pushing these limits.

2.3.1 Maximum Data Rate of a Channel

There are special high-speed modems designed to transmit data over analog lines with a large *bandwidth* (range of frequency). However, the overwhelming majority of modems are designed for the purpose of transmitting data over voice grade circuits on the public telephone network, which have a limited bandwidth. The first segment of a voice grade circuit consists of a twisted pair of copper wires that connects a telephone with the "central office" over a distance of about a mile. A "voice pair" has a bandwidth of 3100 hz, stretching from 300 hz to 3400 hz, with the lower and higher frequencies electronically filtered out.

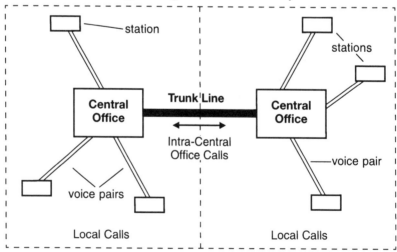

Fig. 2.7 Topology of Telephone Network

Fig. 2.7 (on previous page) shows the basic topology of a telephone network. A voice pair is connected to the local central office, where the switching equipment is located, and the local central office is in turn interconnected to other central offices by trunk lines. An actual call may be routed through more than two central offices if there was no direct interconnecting trunk line or if the direct routing switches were tied up due to abnormally heavy traffic. To give an idea of the switching capacity of a typical central office, a central office can handle all the local calls of a mid-sized town with population of about 25,000.

Voice or data, which is transmitted over the public telephone network, may be routed through one or more switches, transmitted over two or more transmission lines, and often multiplexed onto "trunk lines" that are capable of the simultaneous transmission of many voice grade signals. We refer to this uni-directional path from source to destination as a channel. Although the channel may be complex, it is the "local loop"—the twisted pair that is used to connect a telephone or a modem with the central office—that represents the bottleneck of the channel. This is because of its limited bandwidth of 3100 hz.

In 1934 Harry Nyquist derived an expression for the maximum data rate of a "noiseless" (no interference) channel with a finite bandwidth. Nyquist proved that if a channel was run through a low pass filter with a bandwidth of H it could be completely reconstructed by making $2H$ exact samples per second. If the signal consists of V discrete levels Nyquist's theorem states:

$$\text{maximum data rate} = 2H \log_2 (V) \text{ bits per second}$$

For example, a 3100 hz channel that transmits binary signals (two discrete levels) will have a maximum data rate of 6200 bits per second.

Nyquist's theorem only considered the maximum data rate for a noiseless channel. If random noise is present the maximum data rate deteriorates. The amount of thermal noise is measured by the signal to noise ratio S/N which is usually given in decibels. C. Shannon, who carried Nyquist's work further, came up with the following result which is called Shannon's Law:

$$\text{maximum data rate} = H \log_2 (1 + S/N)$$

For example, a channel which had a signal to noise ratio of 30 dB and a bandwidth of 3100 hz will have a maximum data rate of 31,000 bits per second.

Shannon's law is commonly misunderstood in that it does not say about how many discrete levels are required to achieve the maximum data rate. Obviously, if according to Nyquist's theorem the maximum data rate for a noiseless channel with two discrete levels is 6200 bits per second, on a channel with some noise it will take more than two discrete levels to achieve a data rate of 31,000 bits per second.

Another tool that is used to mathematically ascertain the maximum data rate of a channel is Fourier analysis. Although it is beyond the scope of this book, it has been shown by Fourier analysis that for data rates much beyond 38,400 bits per second there is almost no hope at all of transmitting a recognizable signal on a voice channel, even if the transmission facility is completely noiseless.

2.3.2 Types of Modulation

There are three ways to modulate a carrier signal for the purpose of transmitting binary digital data (see Fig. 2.8 on next page). These three ways are amplitude modulation (AM), frequency modulation (FM), and phase modulation (PM), as shown in Fig. 2.8.

The electronics for amplitude modulation and frequency modulation are pretty straightforward. The amplitude of a carrier can be modulated by adding it to itself with a linear adder with the adder's enable accepting the binary signal, as shown in Fig. 2.9(a) on the next page. The frequency can be varied by feeding the binary input into a voltage controlled oscillator as shown in Fig. 2.9(b).

The electronics of phase modulation are trickier. Fig. 2.10(a), on page 60, shows a product modulator which consists of inductors I1 and

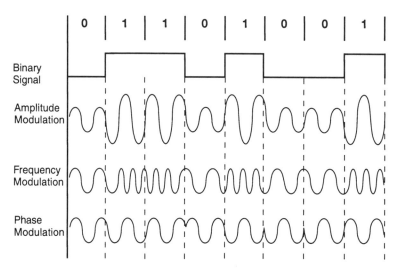

Fig. 2.8 Methods of Modulating a Carrier Signal

I2, and diodes D1-D4. A product modulator relies on the principle of the inductor, which, loosely stated, is: if two coils are in close proximity, a current in one coil will induce a current of the same direction in the other coil. A product modulator also relies on the fact that diodes only allow current to flow in one direction—from high voltage to low.

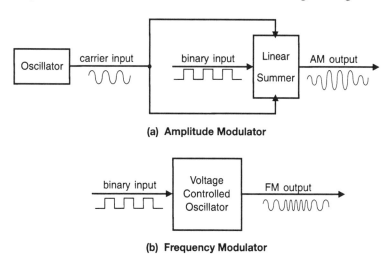

(a) Amplitude Modulator

(b) Frequency Modulator

Fig. 2.9 Block Diagram of AM and FM Electronics

When the binary input is high, as shown in Fig. 2.10(b), diodes 3 and 4 are turned "off" and diodes 1 and 2 are "on" with the resulting carrier output in phase with the carrier input. When the binary input is low, as shown in Fig. 2.10(c), diodes 1 and 2 are turned off and diodes 3 and 4 are on with the carrier output 180 degrees out of phase with the carrier input.

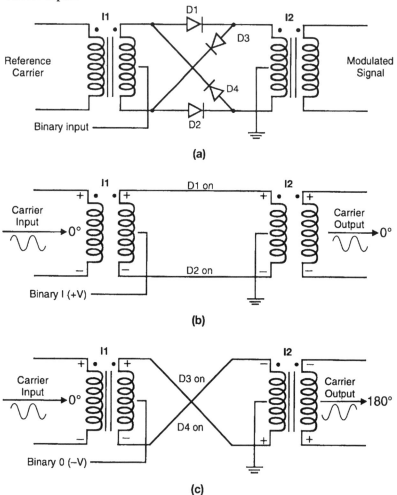

Fig. 2.10 Product Modulator

Most of today's modems use a type of modulation called quadrature amplitude modulation (QAM). QAM works by modulating both the amplitude and the phase. Two variations of QAM are 8-QAM, which encodes three bits in each signal change, and 16-QAM, which encodes four bits in each signal change. Table 2.3 shows how 16-QAM combines ten possible phase angles and three possible voltage levels for the amplitude in order to encode a four bit binary number. The output waveform of a 16-QAM modem is shown in Fig. 2.11.

Binary Inputs				16-QAM Output	
0	0	0	0	0.311 V	- 135°
0	0	0	1	0.850 V	- 165°
0	0	1	0	0.311 V	- 45°
0	0	1	1	0.850 V	- 15°
0	1	0	0	0.850 V	- 105°
0	1	0	1	1.161 V	- 135°
0	1	1	0	0.850 V	- 75°
0	1	1	1	1.161 V	- 45°
1	0	0	0	0.311 V	135°
1	0	0	1	0.850 V	175°
1	0	1	0	0.850 V	45°
1	0	1	1	0.850 V	15°
1	1	0	0	0.850 V	105°
1	1	0	1	1.161 V	135°
1	1	1	0	0.850 V	75°
1	1	1	1	1.161 V	45°

Table 2.3 16-QAM Amplitude Levels and Phase Angles

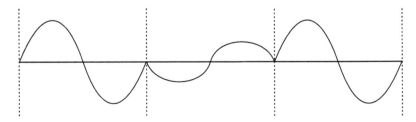

Fig. 2.11 Quadrature Amplitude Modulator

Although we won't show the diagram because of its complexity, a 16-QAM modem works by combining two product modulators and a linear adder in a single circuit. The output of the linear adder is the sum of the outputs of the two product modulators. The inputs of each product modulator is the input carrier and two of the four bits of the binary number which is encoded with each signal change. The four bits are serially clocked into the modem, then the signal is modulated, then the next four bits are clocked in, etc.

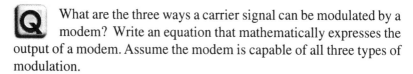

Problem Solving Example:

What are the three ways a carrier signal can be modulated by a modem? Write an equation that mathematically expresses the output of a modem. Assume the modem is capable of all three types of modulation.

Three types of modulation are common.
1. Amplitude modulation.
2. Frequency modulation.
3. Phase modulation.

The carrier signal on the transmission line can be represented by:

$$V(t) = A * \sin (ft * (2\pi + p)), \qquad (1)$$
where $A = 3$, $f = 2000$, $p = 0$, and t = time in seconds

If the values of the amplitude A, the frequency f, and the "phase angle" p are held constant, then a graph of the voltage vs. time would be a smoothly flowing curve—with V(t) varying from +3 V to -3 V and back to +3 V every 1/2000 of a second. Thus, the frequency of this signal would be 2000 Hz. The following are examples of each type of modulation:

- Changing A, while f and p were held constant, would represent amplitude modulation. For example if the amplitude was doubled to A = 6, then V(t) would vary from + 6 V to - 6 V instead of from +3 V to -3 V.
- Changing f, while A and p were held constant, would represent frequency modulation. If f = 1000, the frequency would change to 1000 Hz.

- A sudden change in the phase angle to p = π would result in a sudden phase change of 180 degrees. In other words, if V(t) was rising, it would suddenly be falling at the same rate, and vice versa.

2.3.3 Additional Modem Concepts

Half-Duplex and Full-Duplex

The simplest form of data transmission is *simplex,* which is transmission in one direction from a transmitter to a receiver. Simplex has limited application and is seldom used. Half-Duplex allows transmission in both directions, but not simultaneously. Full-Duplex permits simultaneous transmission and reception of data by two end-stations.

Leased Lines

Much of the signal distorting noise that is generated on public telephone networks is caused by switching gear. "Leased lines" provide a permanent connection between two modems, thus bypassing switching gear. Leased lines have an additional advantage in that they allow faster connections between end-stations by eliminating dial-up time.

Modems transmitting at higher data rates are more prone to errors. In order to reduce the likelihood of high-speed transmission errors, there are two ways leased lines can be "conditioned": type C and type D. There are several categories of both type C conditioning and type D conditioning and the leased line customer can choose one of each.

Type C conditioning reduces the possibility of two types of errors: (1) frequency response, and (2) envelope delay. Frequency response errors are caused by some frequencies losing their strength more than others. Envelope delay errors are caused by some frequencies being delayed more than others. Type C conditioning alleviates both of these problems by insertion of equalizers on the local loop and at the central office.

Type D conditioning guarantees a specified signal-to-noise ratio depending on the type D category selected.

Another advantage of leased lines is that they employ "four-wire" transmission as opposed to the "two-wire" twisted pairs provided by most dial-up lines. Four-wire leased lines offer two independent communication channels, thus facilitating full-duplex transmission.

Synchronization

Modem transmission may be synchronous or asynchronous. Asynchronous transmission begins the transmission of each character with a start bit and ends it with a stop bit (or bits). Synchronous transmission works by first transmitting a training sequence which synchronizes the receiving modem's clock and carrier oscillators. The training sequence is followed by block of data with the receiving modem maintaining synchronization from the normal transitions of the received data.

Synchronous transmission between two modems (DCE equipment) is a different concept from synchronous transfer of data between DTE equipment and DCE equipment (described under the heading "Data Circuit Terminating Equipment (DCE)") which achieves synchronization by using a separate clocking signal.

In general, synchronous modems are faster, partially because they save two or three bits per character by not requiring start and stop bits, and partially because synchronization allows faster bit rates.

Echo Suppressors

Echo is caused by resistance to certain frequencies due to transmission line irregularities. The insertion of echo suppressors into the line improves the quality of voice transmission, but is bad for data. The echo suppressors can be disabled by the answering modem transmitting a 400 millisecond high-pitched tone of about 2500 hz. If there is no period without a carrier signal of more than 100 milliseconds the echo suppressors will stay disabled.

Dial-up Lines

Dial-up lines are inherently more noisy than leased lines. However, the electronics of today's modems (many of which are designed to work on both dial-up and leased lines) have reached a degree of sophistication that allows high data rates on dial-up lines.

Usually dial-up transmission is half-duplex because most dial-up lines are two-wire, with one wire used for transmission and the other used as a reference lead. Full-duplex is possible over two-wire lines, but this requires splitting the bandwidth into two channels so they don't interfere with each other. For example, a data channel in one direction could occupy 300-1800 hz and the data channel in the other direction could occupy 1800-3300 hz. The net result is full-duplex transmission, but at half the bit rate possible with half-duplex.

On the other hand, half-duplex transmission on a two-wire line will have twice the bit rate as full duplex, but slower turn-around time, because the receiver must wait until it is certain the transmitter is finished.

The advantages of dial-up lines are that they are less expensive and they have greater flexibility—they allow a modem to connect with any other modem it can dial.

Baud Rate
So far we have only described transmission rates in terms of bits per second. However, an important concept is the "baud rate." The baud rate is the number of signal changes per unit time. For example, 16-QAM represents four bits with each signal change so a 16-QAM modem with a bit rate of 28,800 will have baud rate of 7,200.

Trellis-Coded Modulation
Trellis-coded modulation (TCM) is one of the reasons that high data rates are achieved even on noisy dial-up lines. The output waveform of a TCM modem appears identical to a QAM modem (see Fig. 2.11), however TCM encodes an extra bit with each signal change for the purpose of error detection and correction. Thus, errors that are encountered by high-speed transmission over noisy lines can be corrected without requiring the retransmission of a block of data. This is called "forward error correction."

2.3.4 Modem Standards

The ITU-T is the most important organization in the area of recommended standards for modems. There are also numerous *de facto* standards that have been created when, for example, a company such as Microcom develops an improved technology and other manufacturers follow suit because it has become commonplace. These *de facto* standard modems are semi-compatible with ITU-T modems in the sense that they have fall-back data rates, modulation methods, and error correction schemes, that fall within the domain of ITU-T recommended standards.

The ITU-T V. series of modem recommended standards is shown in Table 2.4. The frequency shift keying (FSK) represented in the table is similar to the frequency modulation shown in Fig. 2.8. The phase shift keying (PSK) in Table 2.4 is different from the phase modulation shown in Fig. 2.8 in that PSK represents each binary number with a

ITU-T Recomm.	Speed (bps)	Synch Asynch.[1]	Modul.[2]	Duplex[3]	Wire[4]
V.21	300	A	FSK	H, F	2
V.22	600	A	FSK	H, F	2, 4
V.22	1200	A, S	PSK	H, F	2, 4
V.22 bis	2400	A	QAM	H, F	2
V.23	600	A, S	FSK	H, F	2
V.23	1200	A, S	FSK	H, F	2
V.26	2400	S	PSK	H, F	4
V.26	1200	S	PSK	H	2
V.26 bis	2400	S	PSK	H	2
V.26 ter	2400	S	PSK	H, F	4
V.29	9600	S	QAM	H, F	4
V.32	9600	A	TCM, QAM	H, F	2
V.33	14400	S	TCM	H, F	4
V.34	28800	S	TCM	H, F	4
V.34 bis	33600	S	TCM	H, F	4
v.35	4800	S	FM	F	4

NOTES: 1. A = Asynchronous, S = Synchronous
2. FSK = Frequency Shift Keying, PSK = Phase Shift Keying
   QAM = Quadrature Amplitude Modulation, TCM = Trellis Coded Modulation
3. H = Half-Duplex, F = Full-Duplex
4. 2 = 2 wire switched line, 4 = 4 wire leased line

Table 2.4 ITU-T Modem Standards

specific phase angle while the phase modulation in Fig. 2.8 represents the transition (from **0** to **1**, or **1** to **0**) with a phase change.

2.3.5 56 Kbps Modems\c

The new 56 kbps modems take advantage of the fact that there is one less analog to digital A/D conversion when the connection is with an Internet Service Provider (ISP). When a modem is used to download digital data from an ISP, there is no A/D or D/A conversion between the ISP and the central office, because the ISP usually leases a digital T1 line, or an equivalent ISDN interface. This means an ISP connection only requires one D/A conversion, and one A/D conversion, instead of the two of each required when the communication is with another modem. Both of the remaining conversions occur because of the analog local loop – that connects the modem to the central office. When the modem is receiving, it performs the A/D conversion and the central office performs the D/A conversion, and vice versa when the modem is transmitting.

It is the A/D conversion, not the D/A conversion, that actually results in the loss of data – due to quantizing errors. However, if the A/D conversion is performed by the modem, there is less likelihood of data loss. This is because a modem is specially designed to handle digital data, while the A/D converters at the central office are specially designed to digitize voice. Since the telephone companies' equipment does not perform the A/D conversion as well (from the standpoint of data), modems that are capable of receiving at 56 kbps still transmit at the old 28.8/33.6 kbps rates.

There are two competing de facto standards: X2, developed by U.S. Robotics, and k56flex, developed by Rockwell Semiconductors Systems, Inc. The X2 modems are capable of 256 codes per baud, but only use the 128 that are the least effected by noise.

2.4 Multiplexers

Multiplexers allow several data channels to be transmitted on one transmission line. This is accomplished in different ways:

A frequency division multiplexer (FDM) allocates a portion of the bandwidth of the transmission line to each channel. However, FDMs, which multiplex analog signals, are no longer used very much because most multiplexing is now done with digital data. Multiplexing is most useful for expensive, high-capacity long-distance communication lines which have nearly all been converted to digital because digital transmission allows weakened signals to be much more accurately regenerated.

Time division multiplexers (TDMs), which work well with digital data, have extensive applications, especially for wide area networks. This is because WANs employ long distance communication lines— usually leased from a public telephone service provider, but sometimes

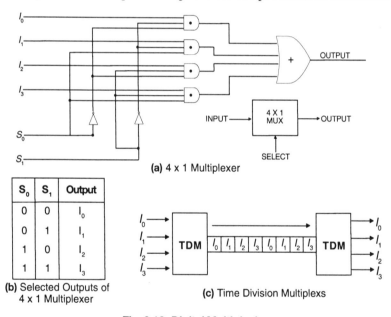

(a) 4 x 1 Multiplexer

S_0	S_1	Output
0	0	I_0
0	1	I_1
1	0	I_2
1	1	I_3

(b) Selected Outputs of 4 x 1 Multiplexer

(c) Time Division Multiplexs

Fig. 2.12 Digital Multiplexing

privately installed. TDMs also are used in hierarchical tree networks to allow several or many terminals to share a communication line with a mainframe computer.

Fig. 2.12(a) (on previous page) shows the logic diagram of a simple 4 × 1 multiplexer. Fig. 2.12(b) shows the binary values of the two select lines, S_0 and S_1, needed to output one of the input lines, I_0-I_3. This is basically all a digital multiplexer is, although this basic logic circuit may be cascaded and combined in various ways in order to multiplex a greater number of input lines. A time division multiplexer will also include a timing device that automatically selects a new input line in a round robin fashion so that each input line is periodically allocated a time slice—as the line to be output. Also, a TDM may include input buffers so that input data will not be lost while an input line is waiting for its time slice.

Although we won't show the logic diagram, a demultiplexer does the same thing, in reverse, as a multiplexer. Digital data, that is transmitted by means of a TDM at the transmitting end, is demultiplexed at the receiving end by means of select lines activated by a timing device. At the receiving end, the N channels of data are received on one incoming line by the demultiplexer, and then are time-divided onto N output lines, as shown in Fig. 2.12(c). Generally, a TDM device is capable of both multiplexing and demultiplexing.

There is also a more sophisticated type of multiplexer called a "statistical multiplexer" that allocates an output channel on the basis of statistically how often an input line requires one.

There is an even more sophisticated device known as a concentrator that is capable of receiving data on different lines at different rates and in different formats and transmitting at one rate in the same format. Concentrators, which usually have software capability, can be programmed to allocate output channels on an as-needed basis, or may have other sophisticated features.

Statistical multiplexers and concentrators are attempts to maximize the use of the available bandwidth of a communication line, which is sometimes wasted by simpler TDMs. A TDM will periodically allocate a data channel to a device, whether or not it has something to transmit.

2.5 Digital Encoding

The parallel digital data that is stored or transferred internally in computers is usually encoded by a high voltage representing binary or logic 1 and a low or zero voltage representing binary or logic 0. For example, 3.7 V to 5.0 V may be interpreted as a binary 1 and 0.0 to 0.6 V may be interpreted as a binary 0 with levels in between only occurring during a rapid transition from low to high.

It is intuitively easiest to think of serial digital transmission as taking the shape of a modified square wave, a good example of which is serial ASCII transmission (see Fig. 1.1 on page 8). However, factors such as power requirements, signal strength over long distances, compatibility with regenerative repeaters, and ease of synchronization often make other forms of digital encoding more desirable.

Fig. 2.13(a) on the next page shows the simplest form of serial digital transmission. This is known as a unipolar (because negative voltage is not used) nonreturn-to-zero (because the voltage is maintained for the entire bit time at one level) encoding scheme.

Fig. 2.13(b) shows a method of digital encoding that represents more than just binary 0 and binary 1 with a single signal element. This is a bipolar non-return-to-zero (BPNRZ) encoding scheme that is known as pulse amplitude modulation (PAM). PAM is often used as the intermediate encoding in the digitization of an analog voice signal (digitization of a voice signal is called "pulse code modulation" (PCM)).

Fig. 2.13(c) shows a popular form of encoding called *Manchester code.* Manchester code, which is bipolar, has two important characteristics: (1) there must be a transition for every binary digit, and (2) the transition for each binary digit is in the center of each signalling element. Manchester code has the advantage that a known transition for every binary digit greatly facilitates clock synchronization. It has the additional advantage of no net DC current, since positive and negative voltage levels balance off exactly. Manchester code has the disadvantage that it requires twice the minimum bandwidth to transmit a binary signal.

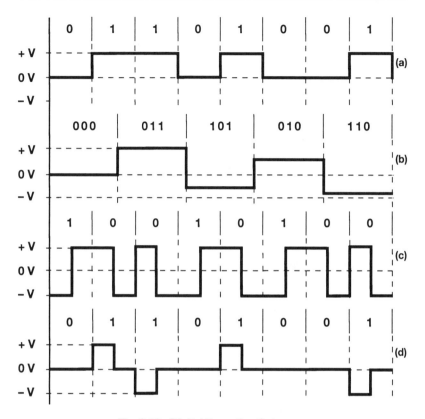

Fig. 2.13   Digital Encoding Schemes

Manchester code is commonly used for LANs with data rates in the multi-megabits per second range. If a cable used for a LAN has a bit capacity of 20 mbps, the data will be transmitted by Manchester code at a maximum rate of 10 mbps, due to the mandatory transition for every bit.

Fig. 2.13(d) shows a form of digital encoding that is often used to transmit digital data over trunk lines of telephone networks. It is called *bipolar return-to-zero – alternate mark inversion* (BPRZ-AMI). The power requirements of BPRZ-AMI are low for four reasons: (1) it is bipolar (bipolar transmission requires only half the power of polar), (2) it is RZ, thus average voltage levels are less, (3) it has a very low DC component, and (4) binary 0 is represented by zero voltage, also reducing average voltage levels.

Alternate mark inversion (AMI) means that "1's" are alternately represented by plus and minus voltage levels. This has the advantage of built in error detection, because any two consecutive positive or negative "1's" is automatically an error.

BPRZ-AMI has the disadvantage that, like Manchester code, it requires twice the minimum bandwidth to transmit a binary signal. It also has the disadvantage that it is not ideal for clock synchronization unless a long string of zeros is prevented from occurring.

BPRZ-AMI is commonly used to transmit digitized speech, and is often the final output of pulse code modulation—after being converted from the intermediate PAM encoding shown in Fig. 2.13(b).

Problem Solving Example:

What is digital encoding? Why is it necessary?
Give examples.

Digital encoding is the conversion of binary data to the discrete values suitable for the transmission technology. It is important, because simply representing zeros with low voltage and ones with high voltage is not always practical.

An example is BPRZ-AMI, which is used by telephone companies for digital signals that travel for miles on trunk lines. BPRZ-AMI represents "1's" with alternate positive and negative voltage and "0's" with zero voltage. The positive and negative "1's" exactly cancel out, so the signal has no DC component. A good analogy is the supplying of AC power by electric utilities, because it travels much farther. A BPRZ-AMI signal is similar to AC in the sense that it has no DC component, allowing it to be transmitted over much greater distances.

2.6 Cables

Cables provide the real transmission medium or physical support for the overwhelming majority of computer network applications. The type of cable best suited for a specific network application depends upon the environment (electromagnetic interference, temperature changes, etc.), required bit rates, available equipment, and other factors.

The three most important types of cable used in LAN installations are twisted pairs, coaxial cable, and optical fiber. The three most important types of cable used in the public telephone network are also twisted pairs, coaxial cable, and optical fiber, although coaxial has largely been displaced by optical fiber and now only has limited use.

MANs and WANs for the most part rely on the public telephone network and therefore use the same transmission media—this holds even for the limited private installations in existence.

2.6.1 Twisted Pairs

Twisted pairs consist of two insulated copper wires (less than a millimeter in diameter) which are twisted to reduce crosstalk or interference between neighboring pairs in the same cable. They are what is referred to as an unbalanced type of circuit because the signal strength is not even from end to end. The signal is carried on one wire with the ground return on the other wire.

The attenuation, or loss of signal strength, is measured in decibels per unit distance. The attenuation is proportional to the square root of the frequency and is also inversely affected by the impedance of the pair. The impedance can be increased by increasing the thickness of the insulation. Data pairs (pairs for the express purpose of transmitting data), which have thicker insulation, will typically have a characteristic impedance of 150 ohms versus 100 ohms for voice pairs. A voice pair will have an attenuation of roughly 10 dB per kilometer at a frequency of 100 kHz while a data pair will have an attenuation of roughly 8.8 dB per kilometer at the same frequency.

To protect against electromagnetic interference, data pairs can be shielded by a very thin metallized tube called a screen and can be further shielded by a braiding of copper wire, as shown in Fig. 2.14 on the next page. It should be noted that although shielding may reduce interference, it does not affect attenuation.

Much of the data transmitted over the public telephone network by modems is over the more error-prone voice pairs, requiring sophisticated modems or slower data rates. This is because there are millions of standard voice pairs in use which connect subscribers to central office switches. However, even unshielded twisted pairs have

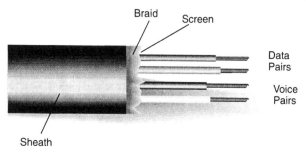

Fig. 2.14 Twisted Pair Cabling

the potential for much higher data rates when used with newer digital technology. One of the motives that the ITU-T had for creating the ISDN (see Chapter 6) standard was to tap the potential of existing voice pairs. With ISDN equipment a telephone line can be used to transmit up to 144 kbps.

ISDN requires a four-wire configuration: two voice pairs in one telephone line—one pair for transmission and the other for reception. Most dedicated leased data lines used with modems are also four-wire, which facilitates full-duplex transmission. However, these are not standard voice pairs but two pairs which have been specially conditioned. In addition, most new wiring to buildings that house businesses is now being done with four-wire lines.

Shielded or unshielded twisted pairs are used to transmit data at much higher rates over shorter distances on local area networks. Data rates from 10 mbps to 16 mbps are common installations using twisted pairs as physical support. The advantages of using twisted pair cabling for LANs are that they are inexpensive and can easily be connected to computers with modular jacks similar to modular jacks plugged into telephones.

2.6.2 Coaxial Cable

Coaxial cable, like twisted pairs, consists of an unbalanced pair of conductors. However, it is configured differently, with an inner core which carries the signal and a surrounding outer conductor which provides the ground return. The outer conductor also shields the inner core from interference.

The outer conductor is either solid or braided and the inner and outer conductors are held in concentric configuration by an insulating material such as Teflon. "Coax" is about as thick as most people's thumbs and has a disadvantage in that it is not very flexible. Another disadvantage is that it is expensive to use. The advantages of coax are: (1) it has high bandwidth, (2) it is useful for networks connected by a passive bus, because it is easy to tap into with "vampire clamps," which pierce the outer conductor, and (3) it is insensitive to different types of electromagnetic interference (i.e., the interference caused by fluorescent lighting).

Coaxial cable was for a long time the most common type of cable in LAN installations, but most newer LANs use twisted pairs.

2.6.3 Fiber Optic Cables

There are basically three types of fiber optic cables as shown in Fig. 2.15 on the next page.

A *multi-mode step index* fiber optic cable, shown in Fig. 2.15(a), consists of a cylindrical core with a refractive index of n_1 surrounded by a *cladding* with a refractive index of n_2 such that $n_2 < n_1$. With the core rays such as *OA* for which the angle *t* is greater than the angle of total internal reflection, are not refracted by the cladding of index n_2. Rays which enter the cable within a limited incidence can follow paths of different lengths within the fiber. This is why such a fiber is described as multimode. The simultaneous existence of these numerous paths, perhaps more than a hundred, causes "modal dispersion" which limits the bandwidth. This type of fiber will have a bandwidth of about 50 mbps.

A reduction of modal dispersion can be achieved by a *multimode graded index* fiber (see Fig. 2.15(b)). The index of refraction increases progressively from n_1 to n_2 from the center to the cladding. The grada-

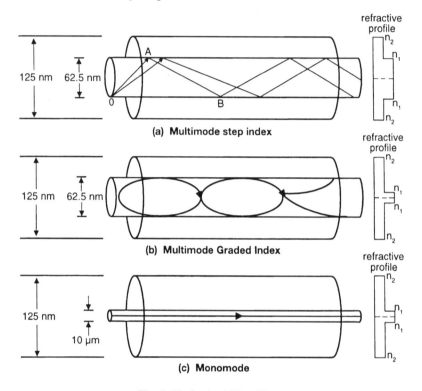

(a) Multimode step index

(b) Multimode Graded Index

(c) Monomode

Fig. 2.15 Optical Fiber Types

tion of the refraction causes the light ray to be deflected towards the axis of the core. Because the length of the trajectories are more constant, the bandwidth is increased by a factor of about ten.

Fig. 2.15(c) shows what is essentially a step index fiber whose core has been decreased to 8-11 micrometers. The result is a single mode of propagation along the axis. For this reason this is called a *monomode* fiber. The bandwidth of this type of fiber is 100 to 1000 times that of multimode step index fiber.

Attenuation per unit length of fiber is due to absorption and a phenomenon called Rayleigh scattering (scattering of light by particles that are small in relation to the wavelength of the light, and in which the intensity of the scattered light varies inversely with the fourth power of the wavelength). The signal strength attenuates at about 1 dB/km which means that repeaters can be spaced at distances of about five miles. Attenuation is particularly low for signals with certain wavelengths: (1) 850 nanometers, (2) 1300 nm, and (3) 1550 nm.

The light sources of optical fibers are either LEDs or laser diodes and the light detectors are either positive intrinsic negative (PIN) photodiodes or "avalanche" type photodiodes.

The operating values and characteristics of the three types of fiber optics in Fig. 2.15 are:

1. A 62.5/125 multimode step index optical fiber with a LED source and operating with a wavelength of 850 nm has an attenuation of 3 dB/km and a bandwidth of about 50 mHz/km.
2. A 62.5/125 multimode graded index optical fiber with a LED source and operating with a wavelength of 1300 nm has an attenuation of 1 dB/km and a bandwidth of about 1 gHz/km.
3. A 10/125 monomode optical fiber with a laser diode source and operating with a wavelength of 1550 nm has an attenuation of 0.3 dB/km and a bandwidth of about 100 gHz/km.

Optical fiber, in addition to its high bit capacity, has very low error rates. Optical fiber has an advantage in that it is immune to electromagnetic interference. Also, it is relatively unaffected by temperature changes. Its light weight allows long sections of cable (up to five miles) to be installed. Optical splices (connections) are difficult, increasing cost of installation, and branches, for the most part are still impractical—this limits the use of fiber to point-to-point links.

The main use of optical fiber is for long distance telephone lines capable of carrying thousands of calls simultaneously and for WANs.

2.7 Digital Public Telephone Services

There are alternatives to using modems for the transmission of computer data over the public telephone network. Most local public telephone companies offer services which allow digital transmission of data directly over the phone lines.

2.7.1 Dataphone Digital Service

The most basic digital service is Dataphone Digital Service (DDS), which, surprisingly enough, was first offered by AT&T in the early 60s. DDS is a leased line service that requires a digital transmit/ receive device called a *Digital Service Unit/Channel Service Unit* (DSU/CSU). Data rates supported by DDS vary from 4800 bps to 64 kbps, although 56 kbps is most commonly used.

DDS requires the removal of loading coils (inductors which lessen analog distortion) from both the local loop and the central office, and the use of regenerative repeaters every few thousand feet. For this reason DDS used to be expensive, but the combination of the development of new, competing digital services, and the competitiveness brought on by telecommunications deregulation has made DDS much less expensive.

DDS transmission has few errors. In fact an accuracy of 99.5% is guaranteed at 56 kbps. However, one of the lingering problems is downtime. This has resulted in subscribers using a relatively new service, switched or dial-up DDS, as a backup, if their leased DDS line goes down.

2.7.2 T1 Lines

For users that require more bandwidth than DDS, there is a type of carrier known as a T1 line. Digital services come in multiples of the DS-0 which is 64 kbps. DS-1 is equivalent to 24 DS-0 channels or 1.544 mbps, and once it is encoded and placed on a specially conditioned wire pair it is a T1 line. T1 lines, which typically consist of 19 gauge copper wire versus typically 24 gauge for voice pairs, have repeaters every 6000 ft. and are shielded by a copper braid. The T1 transmitting and receiving pairs are spaced apart in the cable to reduce interference.

At one time, T1 lines were used as trunk lines connecting central offices about ten to fifty miles apart. Most trunk lines have been replaced by optical fiber cable, but T1 lines are now made available to subscribers requiring dedicated high bandwidth digital links. Subscribers can lease a T1 line, a fraction of a T1 line, more than one T1 line, or for those requiring exceptionally high bandwidth, multiples of T1 lines (see Table 2.5). There has been a greatly increased demand for T1 lines, with total usage growing from 500,000 in 1988, to 1.2 million today.

2.7.3   Digital Subscriber Line (xDSL)

In recent years a new family of technologies has been developed to extend high speed transmission to the local loop. The generic acronym for this family is xDSL. (DSL stands for digital subscriber line.)

High-bit-rate digital subscriber line (HDSL) was developed as a less expensive substitute for T1. HDSL (1.54 mbps) and has had the most commercial success of the xDSL family, but requires two twisted pairs to operate. In many locales it's been standard practice to install business phones with two pairs, so upgrades to HDSL are not that big a deal. On the other hand, residence phones operate with single pairs – making the cost of converting millions of them to HDSL prohibitive.

Asymmetric digital subscriber line (ADSL) operates over single twisted pairs. For this reason, it is being touted as a practical way of extending high-speed digital access to the residence. Since ADSL was originally designed for video on demand – a market that has yet to materialize – it has markedly different downstream and upstream data rates. ADSL is capable of from 1.5 mbps to 9 mbps downstream (central office to residence) and from 16 kbps to 640 kbps upstream. Because of its powerful ability to download video and graphics, ADSL is ideal for the Internet. This fact has led to a revival of ADSL. It has been estimated that 95% of all residences (all of which potential Internet customers) are within ADSL's range of 5.5 km.

ADSL achieves full-duplex transmission on a single twisted pair by means of 1 echo cancellation and 2. frequency division multiplexing (FDM). In most cases, the twisted pairs that connect the residence to the central office are only used to carry a 3.4 kHz voice signal. But these pairs are really capable of supporting a usable bandwidth of about 1.0 mHz. The ADSL technique consists of three basic steps:

1. Of the usable 1.0 mHz spectrum, ADSL allocates the first 25 kHz to voice (to avoid crosstalk).

2. Then, echo cancellation is used to allow a 30 kHz to 200 kHz bandwidth to be used for both upstream and downstream signalling. This allows the entire part of the spectrum from 30 kHz to 1000 kHz to be used for downstream signaling (see Fig. 2.16).

3. Finally, FDM is used to subdivide both the upstream and downstream bandwidth into 4 kHz channels. This allows QAM to be applied to each 4 kHz channels yielding a data rate of 0 to 60 kbps per channel.

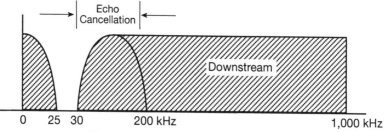

Fig. 2.16 Echo Cancellation Frequency

In theory, since the downstream station is familiar with the signal it is transmitting, it can accurately reconstruct the signal it is receiving from the upstream station by subtracting its own signal. In practice, there is the problem of *echo*. On both ends of the local loop there are what are called hybrids. Hybrids allow a signal to pass in both directions, but hybrids cause a "reflection" of a station's transmitted signal to be "echoed" back. In short there are three kinds of echoes: (1) the near-end echo, (2) the far-end echo (both caused by the hybrids), and (3) an echo caused by the wire itself.

The xDSL family and ISDN use a technique called echo cancellation to minimize the effects. The block diagram of an echo canceller is shown in Fig. 2.17. This device uses this method:

1. Continuously taking samples of its own transmission. These are represented by x(k - n) in Fig. 2.17. Each sample of the transmission has successively more delay, as n increases (the boxes, with the D inside, are delay circuits).

2. Using a feedback circuit to compute the h\v\n\c weighting factors, which are multiplied by the sampled transmitted signal. This estimates each sample's expected echo – depending on how long ago it was transmitted. The feedback circuit is beyond the scope of this book, but it should be pointed out that, because it uses feedback, it is continuously adjusting to current conditions.

3. The estimated echo samples, e(k), are summed and then subtracted from samples of the received signal, r(k).

4. The d(k) is the corrected signal after cancellation.

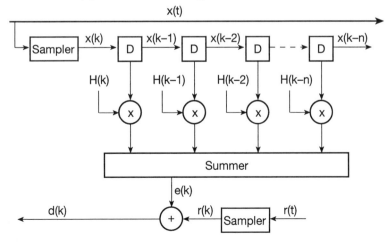

Fig. 2.17 Echo Canceller

2.7.4   Discrete Multitone Transmission (DMT)

Once echo cancellation has made a 1 MHz downstream, and a 170 kHz upstream, channel available, ADSL achieves high data rates by using a technique called *discrete multitone* (DMT). Figure 2.18 depicts a DMT transmitter.

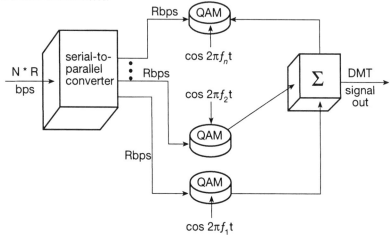

Fig. 2.18   DMT Transmitter

A DMT transmitter consists of a serial-to-parallel converter, a parallel array of QAM modems, and an analog summer, whose purpose is to combine the output from the modems into a single analog signal. The DMT receiver (not shown) divides the downstream input signal by means of a frequency division multiplexer (FDM), then performs the rest of the decoding by doing the same thing in reverse as the transmitter.

Where DMT has proven to be ingenious is that the modems, prior to transmitting data, determine the signal-to-noise ratio at their individual frequencies. Once the signal-to-noise ratios have been determined, each modem selects the appropriate data rate for its channel. The following four criteria are used by the modems to determine the bit rates selected: (1) the fact that the QAM modems are limited to a 4 kHz bandwidth, (2) Shannon's Law, (3) the signal-to-noise ratios of the individual channels, and (4) the increased signal attenuation due to higher frequencies, the bit rates selected for individual channels may be anywhere from 0 kbps to 60 kbps. Assuming a maximum of 256 channels, the potential data rate for ADSL is 15 Mbps.

	ADSL	HDSL	VDSL	SDSL
Data Rate	16 kbps to 640 kbps (upstream) 1.5 Mbps to 9 Mbps (downstream)	1.54 Mbps	1.3 kbps to 2.5 kbps (upstream) 13 Mbps to 52 Mbps (downstream)	1.54 Mbps
Mode	asymmetric	symmetric	symmetric	asymmetric
Frequency	1 Mhz	196 kHz	10 MHz	196 kHz
Signalling	analog	digital	analog	digital
Line Code	DMT	2B1Q	DMT	2B1Q
Twisted Pairs	1	2	1	1
Range 24 gauge (UTP)	3.7 km to 5.5 km	3.7 km	1.4 km	3.7 km

Table 2.5 xDSL Family

Table 2.5 presents a summary of some of the more important xDSL technologies. Unlike ADSL, which uses analog signalling, HDSL and SDSL rely upon digital 2B1Q signalling. The 2B1Q form of signalling represents 2 binary symbols with 1 quaternary symbol and is also used by ISDN, which is covered in Chapter 6, High Speed Networks. The echo cancellation technique is used effectively with both SDSL and ISDN.

2.7.5 Cable Modems

Many residences are wired for high speed access to the Internet services by means of cable modems. A common technique is to install, in a desktop computer, a network interface card (NIC) that would normally be used to connect a computer to a LAN. This method allows the cable to be connected by sophisticated Ethernet (the most common LAN) transceivers, and insures that the computer will be capable of the high speed serial I/O that the NIC provides.

Unfortunately, the technologies used to tap into the cable television network vary so much that the development of standards has been lagging.

2.7.6 The North American Digital Hierarchy

The North American Digital Hierarchy, shown in Table 2.6 below, is made up of the DS series of digital services with an associated T line—the combination of the digital service provided and the actual physical carrier—for each level of service.

DS1 is provided by multiplexing 24 digitized voice channels. A digitized voice channel is created by PCM, which uses a device called a codec to sample an analog voice channel 8000 times a second. Each sample is eight bits, resulting in a data rate of 64 kbps for each voice channel.

Line type	Digital Signal	Bit rate (mbps)	Channel Capacity
T1	DS-1	1.544	24
T2	DS-2	6.312	96
T3	DS-3	46.304	672
T4M	DS-4	274.176	4032
T5	DS-5	560.160	8064

Table 2.6 North American Digital Hierarchy

DS1 transmits a frame every 125 μs—8000 times a second. Since the sample for each of the 24 voice channels is eight bits, a frame is 192 bits plus one bit for synchronization, or 193 bits per frame. The data rate for DS1 can be computed as follows:

$$8000 \text{ frames/second} * 193 \text{ bits/frame} = 1.544 \text{ mbps}$$

The synchronization bit of the odd numbered frames has the bit pattern 01010101. The synchronization bit of the even numbered frames has the bit pattern 0001110.

A superframe combines 12 DS1s into a DS2 frame. DS2 still requires the transmission of signalling and supervisory information. This is done by a technique called "bit robbing." DS2 "robs" every sixth DS1 frame of one bit from each of the eight-bit voice samples, which has little effect on end voice quality. The superframe synchronization pattern, which is the result of combining the even and odd DS1 synchronization bits, is 100011011100.

The lower levels of the North American Hierarchy, such as T1, are similar to river tributaries, with the lower levels multiplexed together to form the higher levels.

Problem Solving Example:

 What is meant by a data channel?

 A data channel can best be described by an example:

Data is transmitted by Modem A—over a twisted pair—to Central Office X. Central Office X is connected to Central Office Y by a T1 trunk line.

At Central Office X, the modem's signal is digitized, and the digital signal is multiplexed with 23 other digital signals. Each of these 24 digital signals represent a channel—any that are digitized data are data channels, and any that are digitized voice are voice channels.

All 24 channels, including the channel that represents Modem A's data, are transmitted—over the T1 line—to Central Office Y. At Central Office Y, the 24 channels are demultiplexed, and Modem A's signal is converted back to analog. The analog signal is then transmitted—over a twisted pair—to Modem B.

The transmission of data from Modem A to Modem B is a data channel. It may have been multiplexed for transmission on a T2 trunk line (96 channels) or a T3 trunk line (672 channels), or another kind of trunk line. It may have been routed through more than one central office, if a direct connection were not available. But the concept is still the same. Even if the signal transmitted from the subscriber to the central office, is digital rather that analog—as in the case of DDS, or ISDN, or a dedicated T1 carrier—the concept of a data channel is still the same: the transfer of data between two DCE devices over one of many various types of transmission lines.

CHAPTER 3

The Data-Link Layer

This chapter will discuss data-link layer concepts in general, and relate them to high level data-link control (HDLC). HDLC could be considered the most widely used data-link protocol, if all the minor variations closely related to HDLC were included. The reader should, however, bear in mind that other protocols are used for the data-link layer. For example, the data-link layers of LANs are divided into two sublayers: (1) the upper sublayer logical link control (LLC), which is closely related to HDLC, and (2) the lower sublayer, medium access control (MAC), which varies from LAN to LAN. The MAC sublayer will be covered in Chapter 5, Local Area Networks.

The data-link layer is responsible for establishing a communication link over a physical channel. This is accomplished by the transmission of command and response protocol data units (PDUs). PDUs are referred to as frames at the data-link level.

The data-link layer transmits data which is transparent both to itself and to its peer on the receiving station. The data to be transmitted is received from the network layer in the form of service data units (SDUs). The SDUs become the data portion of the link layer protocol data units (LPDUs) when a header, and usually a trailer, is added. The header contains protocol control information (PCI) and the trailer contains error detection information. The data-link layer at the receiving station processes the LPDU by first checking for errors and then by examining the PCI. If all the PCI contains is a command to pass the data to its own network layer, which is often the case, then the header and trailer are stripped off and the SDU is passed to the network layer.

Prior to transmission, the LPDU is "framed" by appending a flag field (a unique bit sequence) both in front of and after the LPDU, which serves as the frame's starting and ending delimiters. Because the data-link layer is the only one of the six upper OSI layers that transmits data over a physical link, and because the physical layer is concerned only with a series of bits, the data-link layer is the only layer which frames its PDUs—hence the unique term frame for an LPDU.

The data-link layer has no provision for dividing the data units prior to transmission, called "segmenting." Neither is there a provision for combining data units, called "reassembly." Thus, there is a one-to-one correspondence between each SDU received from the network layer and each frame transmitted by the data-link layer.

LPDUs contain address information. If there are only two stations on the link there is no need for an address field. But, for example, local area networks will often have multiple stations on the same link, thus the receiver needs to be identified. There are also cases when the sender needs to be identified, which will be discussed in the next section.

The data-link layer nearly always operates with bit-oriented protocols. An example of an older, seldom used, byte-oriented protocol is IBM's binary synchronous communications (BSC). This protocol begins a transmission with several SYN characters (see Table 1.1 on page 6). This is followed by an SOH (start of header), then by the header field, then the data field, and finally by a ETB (end of transmission block). The problem with this protocol is the possible random occurrence of control characters in the data field. One solution is the insertion of a DLE (data-link escape) before every occurrence of a control character in the data field. This method is cumbersome and can add unnecessarily to overhead.

Bit-oriented protocols do not use control characters. But there is still a chance that the starting and ending delimiter (the flag) could occur either in the data field, or in one of the other fields—the address field, for example. To prevent the random occurrence of the flag, in one of the other fields, a relatively fast and efficient technique called "bit-stuffing" is used. For example, HDLC frames its LPDUs with flag fields containing 01111110. The transmitter prevents any random occurrence of the flag by inserting (stuffing) a 0 any time it detects five consecutive ones. The data-link layer of the receiver strips off the delimiter flags and removes the extra zeros, and what is left is the original LPDU.

Problem Solving Example:

Q Why are data-link PDU's referred to as frames? What is the significance of this in regard to the technique of bit stuffing? Why is bit stuffing considered more efficient than byte, or character, stuffing?

A Data-link PDU's are referred to as frames because they are "framed" by flag fields that serve as starting and ending delimiters. If a flag field occurs at random in one of the non-flag fields, a 0-bit is stuffed so the random occurrence won't be interpreted as the ending delimiter.

Bit stuffing is considered more efficient than byte stuffing because only one bit is required, reducing overhead.

3.1 Error Checking

The data-link layer is responsible for transforming an error prone physical link into a relatively error free logical link for the network layer. The type of error checking done by the data-link layer is usually accomplished by a hardware or firmware implementation. Error checking performed by hardware is very fast, and although the percentage of errors detected is not ideal, it is still very high. The network layer usually does further error checking on data transmitted to or from intermediate nodes, usually by implementing a software checksum. The transport layer performs further software error checking on data transmitted between end-stations.

The data-link layer doesn't have to catch every error, because the upper layers should catch the errors it missed. However, it should detect virtually all errors, and this process should be fast and efficient. For reasons already stated, the most common form of data-link error checking is cyclic redundancy checking (CRC).

With CRC checking the message polynomial $G(x)$ is essentially divided by a generator polynomial $P(x)$, the quotient is discarded, and the remainder is truncated so that it has the same number of bits as the $P(x)$. It is then appended to the message as the block check sequence (BCS). When performed by the data-link layer, the message polynomial $G(x)$ is the LPDU, not including the flag and check fields, and the BCS is called the frame check sequence (FCS).

In the United States the most common CRC code is CRC-16 which is identical to the V.41 standard recommended by the ITU-T. The generator polynomial is represented by:

$$P(x) = x^{16} + x^{12} + x^5 + x^0$$

where $P(x)$ is a binary number and $x = 1$,

such that $P(x) = 10001000000100001$.

Prior to the CRC division the $G(x)$ is multiplied by the highest term of the $P(x)$. When CRC division is performed the subtraction sub-operation is different from standard arithmetic in that:

1. No borrowing is performed.
2. The result is an exclusive-or (XOR) function, with each corresponding bit XORed.
3. The result of each XOR is a 1 if and only if one, but not both of the corresponding bits is a 1.

The following example shows how the FCS would be generated for a simpler polynomial.

Example

Compute the FCS for the following data and CRC generating polynomials:

data $G(x) = x^7 + x^4 + x^3 + x^2 + x^1 + x^0$ or   10011111

CRC $P(x) = x^5 + x^4 + x^2 + x^0$ or   110101

Solution

First $G(x)$ is multiplied by the highest degree term in the generator polynomial $P(x)$

$$x^5 (x^7 + x^4 + x^3 + x^2 + x^1 + x^0) = x^{12} + x^9 + x^8 + x^7 + x^6 + x^5$$
$$= 1001111100000$$

```
                    111110101
        110101|10011111000000
               110101
               100101
               110101
                100001
                110101
                101000
                110101
                 111010
                 110101
                  111100
                  110101
                   100100
                   110101
                    10001  = CRC or FCS
```

CRC-16 is carried out in a way similar to the example above except that the polynomial $P(x)$ and the FCS are of degree sixteen rather than degree five.

When CRC error checking is used by the data-link layer, the transmitter generates a FCS, stores it in the FCS field of the LPDU, then transmits the frame. The receiver performs the same operation with the same generator polynomial $P(x)$ on the received frame, minus the flag and FCS fields. Then the FCS field is compared to the FCS generated by the receiver. If no match is found then a retransmission is requested.

CRC-16 error checking, when carried out according to the ITU-T standard, can detect:

1. All single errors.
2. All errors when $G(x)$ contains an odd number of bits.
3. All double errors.
4. All burst errors of length less than sixteen.
5. 99.997% of burst errors of length seventeen.
6. 99.998% of burst errors of length greater than seventeen.

Cyclic redundancy checking can easily be implemented in hardware with the combination of shift registers and XOR gates. Fig. 3.1 shows the block diagram of a circuit capable of generating a CRC-5 FCS. Note that for every binary digit in the generating polynomial that is a "1" there is a XOR gate.

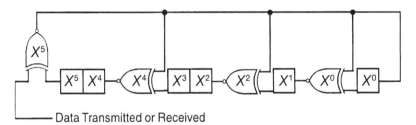

Data Transmitted or Received

Fig. 3.1   CRC Generating Circuit for $P(x) = x^5 + x^4 + x^1 + x^0$

CRC checking is also capable of correction of single errors if:

$$2^r > l + r + 1$$
where r equals the degree of $P(x)$,
and l equal the length, in bits, of $G(x)$.

CRC error correction has limited application for correction of single errors of header information. For example, it is used to correct single bit error of ATM header cells, which will be discussed in Chapter 7, The Internet.

Problem Solving Example:

Q Why is the data link layer usually the only layer that adds a trailer as well as a header? Also, why is the data link layer one of the only two layers that is partially implemented in hardware? Tie the two concepts together.

A The data-link layer adds a trailer, usually a CRC polynomial, for the purpose of error checking. If the CRC follows the part of the frame that is being checked, CRC error checking can be efficiently handled by hardware. Thus, the data-link layer adds the CRC as a trailer to facilitate hardware error checking.

3.2 High-Level Data-Link Control (HDLC)

High-level data link control (HDLC) was developed by the International Standards Organization in the late 1970s with IBM contributing to HDLC's development with its own link layer protocol, SDLC, which is a subset of HDLC.

3.2.1 Classes of Procedures

There are three possible types of stations on an HDLC link:

1. **Primary** stations that issue commands.
2. **Secondary** stations that issue responses.
3. **Combined** stations that issue both command and response.

There are two possible HDLC modes of operation:

1. **Unbalanced operation** - This mode of operation is used with one primary station and one or more secondary stations.
2. **Balanced operation** - This mode of operation is used with two or more combined stations.

An HDLC link can be initialized to two possible data transfer modes:

1. **Normal response mode** - In this mode, a secondary station may only transmit after a primary station has polled it.

2. **Asynchronous response mode** - In this mode, either a primary or secondary station may transmit whenever it finds the link idle.

Three "Classes of Procedure" have been defined for HDLC:

1. Unbalanced Operation in Asynchronous Response Mode (UAC).
2. Unbalanced Operation in Normal Response Mode (UNC).
3. Balanced Operation in Asynchronous Response Mode (BAC).

The first two classes of procedure, UAC and UNC, are used primarily for networks with hierarchical tree topologies and a host computer controlling a number of simpler stations. These types of networks have become relatively less important as the trend towards distributed computer networks has continued.

Here are two examples of how the HDLC protocol's third class of procedure (BAC) might be used:

1. as the link access procedure of a local area network with several or many computers, and each one operating as a combined station.
2. as the link access procedure of a wide area packet switching network with only a single link connecting two intermediate nodes—with both operating as a combined station.

It is important to note that when the term asynchronous is used in describing the classes of procedures UAC and BAC, it does not mean asynchronous in the same sense as the asynchronous transmission of bytes described in Section 1.1.1 on page 6. The asynchronous transmission of bytes (usually), requiring start and stop bits, is a physical layer level protocol. HDLC is a bit-oriented protocol whose frames are transmitted synchronously, as a series of bits, at the physical layer level. However, at the level of the data-link layer—what is referred to as the "logical link"—communication may still be synchronous or asynchronous.

We will present two examples, in the next section, that demonstrate the difference between synchronous and asynchronous communication at the data-link level.

3.2.2   The HDLC Frame

Fig. 3.2 shows the basic format of an HDLC frame. It was designed to work with a multiplicity of different kinds of links, as we will describe.

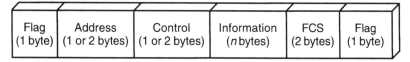

| Flag
(1 byte) | Address
(1 or 2 bytes) | Control
(1 or 2 bytes) | Information
(*n* bytes) | FCS
(2 bytes) | Flag
(1 byte) |

Fig. 3.2   HDLC Frame

The Address Field

The first bit of the address field is used to indicate whether the address field is one or two bytes. If the first bit of the address field is a zero, then the address field is one byte and there are 127 possible addresses of stations on the link. If all but the first bit is a one, then it is a broadcast frame intended for every station on the link. If the first bit is a one, then the address field is two bytes and there are 32,768 possible stations.

On a link with combined stations, the address field contains the address of the receiving station if it is a command, and the address of the sending station if it is a response. On a point-to-point link obviously addresses are not needed to identify the sending or receiving station, but the address field is still used to differentiate between commands and responses.

The Control Field

As shown in Fig. 3.3 on the next page, the control field is formatted differently for each of the three types of frames. Each station maintains wrap-around counters how many frames—not counting unnumbered frames—it has transmitted (N_s) or received (N_r). The receive count in an information frame contains the number of the next expected frame.

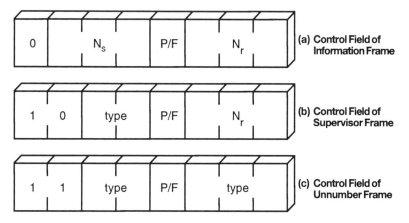

(a) Control Field of Information Frame

(b) Control Field of Supervisor Frame

(c) Control Field of Unnumber Frame

Fig. 3.3 Control Field of HDLC Frame

Acknowledgments can be sent in two ways. The first is by the receiver transmitting back an information frame, with the receive count informing the sending station that all frames up to the receive count minus one have been received and are error free. If the receive count is equal to or less than the send count of the sender, than a sequence or an FCS error has been found. This means the receiver has discarded the frame indicated by the receive count plus any frames that may have followed. Thus, the sending station will have to decrement its send counter to that earlier point and begin retransmitting.

Command	Description	Frame Type
RR	Receive ready	S
RNR	Receive not ready	S
REJ	Reject all frames $\geq$ receive count	S
SREJ	Selectively reject frame designated by receive count	S
SAB(E)	Set asynchronous balanced mode (extended)	U
UA	Unnumbered acknowledge	U
DM	Disconnect mode	U
FRAMR	Frame reject	U

Table 3.1 Selected HDLC Commands

The second way of sending acknowledgments is by sending a supervisor frame with either a REJ (reject/binary 10) or a SREJ (selective reject/binary 11) in the type bits of the control field (see Table 3.1 on previous page). If the control field contains a REJ, then all frames from the receive count on are rejected, otherwise just the referenced frame is rejected. This method is only used with full-duplex transmission.

Flow control is achieved by the windowing technique. If one byte control fields are used then the maximum window size is seven. If two byte control fields are used then the send and receive counts are represented by seven bit binary numbers, thus the maximum window size is 127. This, of course, requires sufficient buffers for both the transmitter and receiver to hold incoming and outgoing frames until they have been processed.

The P/F bit is used by the primary station, in classes of procedures UAC and UNC, to "poll" secondary stations—to indicate to the secondary station that it must acknowledge the frame. In all three classes of procedure the P/F bit is used to indicate the "final" frame of a series of information frames.

The unnumbered frames are used to send commands or responses (see Table 3.1) that can not be acknowledged by receive counts. They must be acknowledged by responses. For example, a station may send the SABM (E) command—set asynchronous response mode balanced with extended (two byte) control fields. The receiver may acknowledge with the UA response (unnumbered acknowledgment), or the FRAMR response (frame reject) if the command is invalid because it has insufficient buffer space to operate with extended control fields.

Other HDLC Frame Fields

The data field can contain any number of bytes with the maximum number left as an issue for network management. However, the FCS, which is generated by a CRC-16 polynomial, works best with a data field of about a hundred bytes.

The flag fields contain the bit sequence 01111110, as described earlier.

3.2.3 Examples of HDLC

Fig. 3.4 shows an example of the class of procedure UNC with communication between a primary and a secondary station. When the primary station transmits the information frame with a send count of three it also polls the secondary station by setting the poll (P) bit. At this point the secondary station responds with an acknowledgment of the last error-free information frame it has received. The information frame sent back to the primary station contains a receive count of four (the number of the expected next frame), and thus acknowledges the successful reception of frames with send counts up to three. Also, the secondary station indicates, by setting the final (F) bit, that the primary station may resume transmission. In this way both sides are kept in synchronism, which is why the term synchronous is used when describing this class of procedure.

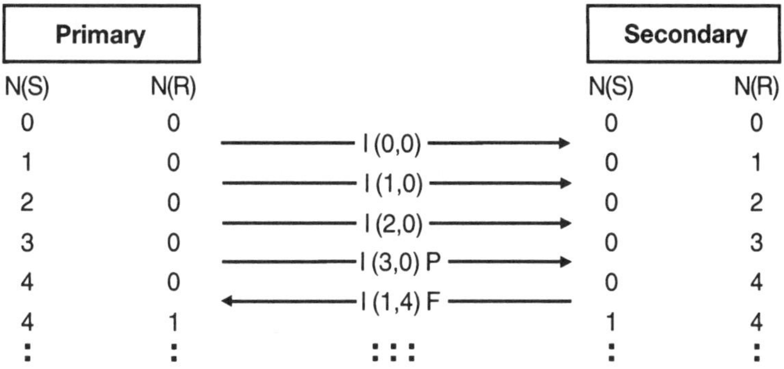

Fig. 3.4 Operation of Synchronized Counters

An example of class of procedure BAC is depicted in Fig. 3.5 on the next page. Full-duplex transmission is used, as shown in Fig. 3.5, resulting in the receive counter of Station B running behind the send counter of Station A. This is because B has not yet received the last frame transmitted by A. Since this type of transmission is obviously not kept in synchronism, the term asynchronous is used when describing this class of procedure.

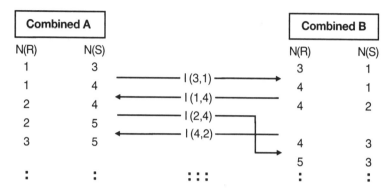

Fig. 3.5 Operation of Non-Synchronized Counters

3.2.4   Time-Outs

If a station transmits a frame and there is no acknowledgment or response, there must be some way for the station to recover. Data-link protocols provide for setting a limit on the time it will wait for a response, by allowing for a timer to be set. When the time-out occurs, the transmitting station can interrogate the intended receiving station by sending it unnumbered command frames. Perhaps it is in disconnect mode and will send back the unnumbered response DM (see Table 3.1). In this case it will only respond to mode setting commands such as SABM (also see Table 3.1).

3.2.5   Applications of the HDLC Protocol

A version of HDLC is recommended by the ITU-T as the link layer protocol for X.25 packet switching networks. The X.25 standard is in widespread use, especially in Europe. The version of HDLC that is used for the X.25 standard is called *link access procedure-balanced* (LAP-B).

Another version of HDLC called LAP-D is used, by ISDN, for the communication between user nodes (stations on the public telephone network) and the central office. The ISDN standard was created by the ITU-T for the eventual purpose of providing integrated services of voice and digital data over a worldwide telephone network.

As mentioned in the introduction, a mode of operation of HDLC forms the *logical link control* (LLC) upper sublayer of the data-link layer of local area networks. The lower sublayer called "medium access control" (MAC), depends on the type of LAN and will be discussed in Chapter 5. This should provide some insight as to why the term "high" in high level data-link control.

Also, SDLC, which is the data-link protocol for IBM's System Network Architecture, is generally considered a subset of HDLC.

Problem Solving Example:

 What is the significance of HDLC? Why do we study the nuts and bolts of HDLC when we study the data-link layer?

 We study high level data control (HDLC), because it is used so much. The upper data-link sublayer of the IEEE 802 series of standardized LANs is a good example.

CHAPTER 4

The Network Layer

The Open Systems Interconnection Reference Model has two forms: (1) the Direct Model, and (2) the Network Model (see Fig. 1.11 on page 22). The Direct Model provides a reference for networks which have a direct communications link between any two stations. The Network Model provides a reference for more complex networks which require end-systems to communicate through at least one intermediate node. The network layer provides those functions that are necessary for the routing and switching of packets (NPDUs) that are transmitted between end-stations—through intermediate nodes.

4.1 Connection-Oriented vs. Connectionless Network Operation

Many readers will be familiar with logging on to a multi-user system by typing in a user name and a password. The host responds by granting a session, and at this point a connection has been established.

The advantage of a connection-oriented operation is that a lot of work gets done during a connection establishment that doesn't have to be re-done with each transaction. A connection nearly always is established at some level, even if it is only an association between applications. At the network layer both connection-oriented and connectionless operation is quite common. There are advantages to both, which will be discussed.

4.1.1   Connection-Oriented Network Operation

The OSI Reference Model provides for both a connectionless and a connection-oriented operation between two end-systems. When a connection is established across a network, the service provided by the network layer is the relatively error-free, sequential delivery of transport layer data. The network layer provides this service by performing the following operations:

1. establishing a *virtual circuit* across a network. The difference between a switched circuit and a virtual circuit is that a switched circuit is established by electronic switches, while a virtual circuit utilizes the intermediate nodes' software and *routing tables* to maintain an end-to-end connection.
2. checking for sequence errors at both end-systems, and at intermediate nodes. If NPDUs are out of order, they are reordered. If an NPDU is lost, a retransmission is requested.

4.1.2   Virtual Circuit Routing Tables

When a network layer receives a request from the transport layer to establish a connection, it builds an NPDU which contains: (1) the address of the other end-system, or host, and (2) the *virtual circuit number* (VCN). When this NPDU is transmitted, a virtual circuit is created on the network—a specific route from the source host, through the intermediate nodes, to the destination host. Thereafter, transmitted NPDUs contain only virtual circuit numbers. Virtual circuit numbers are used to relay packets to each successive node along the route. Virtual circuit numbers are smaller than network addresses, reducing overhead, because each switching node only needs to uniquely identify the devices that are directly attached to it rather than every device on the entire network.

Fig. 4.1(a) on the next page shows an example of a switching network, Fig. 4.1(b) shows the virtual circuits in effect, and Fig. 4.1(c) shows the routing tables maintained by the intermediate nodes, or "switching nodes." The switching nodes are labeled SN1-SN5. The first NPDU transmitted when a connection is made is called the "setup packet." The setup packet causes the switching nodes to make entries in their routing table—these entries are based upon the information contained in the address and virtual circuit number fields of the setup packet.

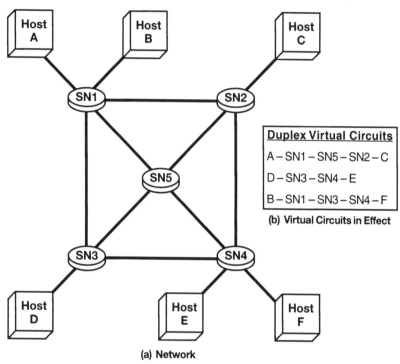

Duplex Virtual Circuits

A – SN1 – SN5 – SN2 – C

D – SN3 – SN4 – E

B – SN1 – SN3 – SN4 – F

(b) **Virtual Circuits in Effect**

(a) **Network**

Switching Node 1

In		Out	
Node	**VCN**	**Node**	**VCN**
A	0	SN5	1
B	0	SN3	2
SN5	1	A	0
SN3	2	B	0

Switching Node 5

In		Out	
Node	**VCN**	**Node**	**VCN**
SN1	1	SN2	4
SN2	4	SN1	1

(c) **Routing Tables**

Switching Node 2

In		Out	
Node	**VCN**	**Node**	**VCN**
SN5	4	C	3
C	3	SN5	4

Fig. 4.1 Assignment of Virtual Circuit Numbers Across a Complex Network

Since more than one host may be connected to an intermediate node and since each host may use the same virtual circuit number when establishing a connection, the switching node must make two VCN entries: (1) the VCN received from the host, and (2) the VCN it will pass on to the next switching node (the lowest one that is not in use by itself). Note that the routing table of SN1 has the same incoming VCN for both Host A and Host B, but different outgoing VCNs.

As the virtual circuit is established across the network, the virtual circuit numbers that will be used for each "hop" are entered into the intermediate node's routing tables, and are often different than the VCNs that were entered at the previous hop. This ultimately results in the nominated host associating a VCN with this connection that is usually different from the VCN that the initiating host is transmitting (see Fig. 4.1(c)). This, however, doesn't make any difference, because it will "appear" to each host that it is using the same VCN.

Since each virtual circuit is full-duplex, the same routing tables may be used for transmission in both directions.

The last packet that is transmitted, which causes the end-systems to disconnect, is called the clear packet and also causes the switching nodes to delete the virtual circuit data from their routing tables.

4.1.3   Connectionless Network Operation

During the process of connection establishment, the entities of a given layer change state from "idle," to an in-between state during which the entities of that layer will not act upon further requests, and then finally, when the connection is made, to a state of "readiness."

By contrast, a connectionless mode of operation does not regard the entities of a given layer to be idle, but always in a "ready" state. A connection-oriented transport service may operate with a connectionless network layer, leading to the type of operation shown in Fig. 4.2 on the next page.

Network layer packets transmitted across a connectionless network are called datagrams. Datagrams are not acknowledged, it's just assumed that they will reach their destination—the so-called "send and pray" method of transmission. When datagrams are used the complete address has to be included in every packet header, rather than just the setup packet—adding to overhead.

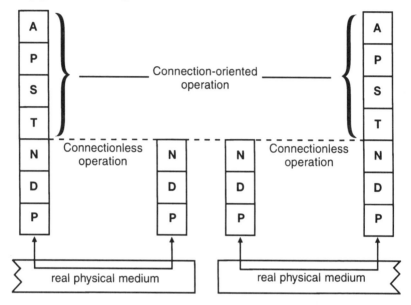

Fig. 4.2 Connectionless Network Layer Operation

When the virtual circuit model is used—which requires that a connection be established—packets arrive in sequence and there is no danger of packets being lost because positive and negative acknowledgments are used to prevent this. When datagrams are used to transmit messages, packets may arrive out of sequence because every datagram is routed independently. Also, the sender has no way of knowing that the packet (the datagram) was received because acknowledgments are not used.

Despite the disadvantages of overhead, reliability, and out-of-sequence delivery, datagrams are usually faster because they allow more flexible routing. A connectionless network layer protocol which transmits datagrams usually operates in conjunction with a connection-oriented transport layer (see Fig. 4.2). In this situation, the transport layer is responsible for sequencing, acknowledgments, and error control.

Problem Solving Example:

 Q What is the difference between a virtual circuit and a switched circuit?

A A switched circuit is established by physical switches. An example is the telephone company responding to a dial call by establishing an end-to-end path for the signal by means of electronic switches. A virtual circuit is established across a network by switching nodes making entries in their routing tables. After the virtual circuit is established, packets are forwarded along the correct path as a result of switching nodes consulting their routing tables.

Virtual and physical circuits can both be used for both voice and data, although voice over virtual circuits is still in an experimental stage.

4.2 Routing Algorithms

Two types of network operation have been described: the virtual circuit model and the connectionless datagram model. With the former, intermediate nodes are usually referred to as switching nodes or *switches,* while with the latter they are usually referred to as routers. This section will concentrate on routing algorithms commonly used on the Internet, which rely on the Internet Protocol (IP) for the connectionless delivery of datagrams.

Although how switching nodes select the route for a virtual circuit won't be discussed here, that does not mean that the routing algorithms are necessarily different. The most important difference is that virtual circuits use the same route from connection establishment until connection release, while datagrams are routed independently.

There are four major classes of routing algorithms: (1) *Static,* (2) *Quasi-static,* (3) *Centralized,* and (4) *Distributed Adaptive.*

1. **Static Routing** - With static routing, tables are either distributed by a central station or are entered manually. The tables, which contain the information used to make routing decisions,

need to be recomputed in the event of failure. For this reason, static routing is not used by major protocols.

2. **Quasi-Static Routing** - Quasi-static routing tables include precalculated alternatives that allow for node failure. Quasi-static routing is used by many packet switching networks. The disadvantage of quasi-static routing is that tables have to be recomputed when new nodes are added.

3. **Centralized Routing** - Centralized routing requires network nodes to transmit information to a network controller, which computes the best current routes and passes them back to the routers. This can lead to excessive traffic in the vicinity of the controller, and a single point of failure can also disrupt the network.

4. **Distributed Adaptive Routing** - This is the type of routing that is most common. Routing information is distributed throughout the network and routing tables are periodically updated to adjust to network changes. There are two types of algorithms that are used: (1) Distance-vector, and (2) Link-state. We will present examples of each of these two types in the next two sections.

4.2.1 Routing Information Protocol (RIP)

The Routing Information Protocol (RIP) was originally developed for Xerox's XNS networks, but was later adapted by the University of California at Berkeley for use by Novell and by the ARPANET. The ARPANET, at the time, was the administrator of the Internet. RIP has its limitations, one of which is that it is only capable of routing packets across networks with a maximum of 15 hops. However, RIP is still in widespread use on many of the networks that make up the Internet.

The Internet uses the TCP/IP suite of protocols, which includes RIP. An interconnected network that uses the TCP/IP suite, but is not connected to the Internet, is referred to as an internet. The network shown in Fig. 4.3 on the next page would work well with TCP/IP. More about the Internet's topology and internetworking mechanisms will be explained in the next section and in Chapter 7, The Internet, but for now the network in Fig. 4.3 can be considered an internet, or more specifically as an independent network that uses the RIP routing protocol.

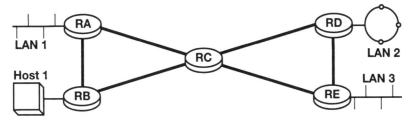

Fig. 4.3 Independent TCP/IP Network

The RIP protocol provides a connectionless datagram type of delivery service. Packets may arrive out of order, or may sometimes be lost altogether. When RIP is used for routing, it is up to higher protocol layers to establish an end-to-end connection and guarantee the integrity of data.

RIP relies on a distance-vector algorithm. RIP, like most distance-vector protocols, measures cost by counting hops. How routers learn the cost, or distance, to every destination on the network is described by the following:

1. Routers periodically, about every 30 seconds, communicate— "advertise"—all of the information stored in their routing tables, but only to their immediate neighbors.

2. It might seem that at first the routers would have no information to advertise, but since they share a link with every router they are connected to, they do have some information. Table 4.1(a) on the next page shows the information stored in the routing table of Router A of Fig. 4.3, after the first 30 second interval. Table 4.1 includes Internet type addresses, which will be discussed in Chapter 7.

4. After the second update occurs, after a total of 60 seconds, every router on the network has acquired the cost, in terms of hops, to every other router—and the algorithm has

converged. Table 4.1(b) shows the routing table of Router A, after convergence has occurred. It would take an additional hop to reach a specific host on one of the LANs. Routers only include in their tables those hosts which are "reachable" in one hop.

Destination Network	Hops	Next Hop
129.7.0 (Host 1)	1	129.7.52
139.22.0 (RC)	1	139.22.45

(a) Table of Router A after 1st Update

Destination Network	Hops	Next Hop
129.7.0 (Host 1)	1	129.7.52
139.22.0 (RC)	1	139.22.45
164.18.0 (LAN 2)	2	139.22.45
182.71.0 (LAN 3)	2	139.22.45

(b) Table of Router A after Convergence

Table 4.1   Routing Tables of Router A

Actually, the example network shown in Fig. 4.3 is quite small compared to actual networks that use RIP, so the convergence time could be considerably longer. This could lead to difficulty when the network topology changes, especially if a router goes offline or a link goes down. For example, the convergence time for an RIP network with the maximum number of 15 hops would be 450 seconds. That is a long time for packets to be lost due to incomplete routing tables.

Triggered Updates

One solution to the problem of slow convergence is "triggered updates." For example, if Router A learns that Router B has gone off-line it will immediately advertise this to its neighbors, Routers B and C. Router C will then immediately communicate the change to Router D. By not waiting for the periodic 30 second update, the change in network topology becomes known much faster. Also, since triggered updates only include changes, as opposed to the entire routing table, updates do not contribute to excessive network traffic.

Unfortunately, a router does not assume that its neighbor has gone off-line until it has not been heard from for a time-out interval of about 180 seconds. This is one of the problems with RIP. The triggered update process greatly increases the speed of informing routers of network changes, but it takes a while for the process to begin.

Split Horizon

When a router informs its neighbors that another router has gone off-line, it advertises that the distance to that link is infinity. The definition of infinity with the RIP protocol is greater than 15 hops. However, there are situations that can cause the distance between routers to be erroneously considered to be less than infinity.

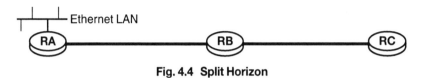

Fig. 4.4 Split Horizon

Fig. 4.4 shows three routers with an Ethernet (a shared bus type of LAN) attached to the router on the left. If the left router goes down, the center router will eventually time-out and enter the distance to the Ethernet as infinity. However, if soon after that it receives the right router's periodic update, it will enter the distance to it as three, because it will assume the right router has a backdoor route to that link. When it is time for the center router's periodic update, the right router will enter four as the distance to the left router, because the only route it knows is through the center router. Eventually both routers will count to infinity, greater than 15, and the link will no longer be considered reachable. But in the meantime they will mistakenly try to route packets to the Ethernet.

Distance-vector protocols employ a technique known as "split horizon" to avoid the "count to infinity" problem. If split horizon is used, a distance router will not advertise the cost to a network or to a link, if it originally received the information on that link. There is a variation of split horizon known as "poison reverse" whereby a router will advertise the distance as infinity, if it received the information on that link. Poison reverse is considered more unambiguous than split horizon.

4.2.2   Open Shortest Path First Protocol (OSPF)

The Open Shortest Path First (OSPF) protocol has significant advantages over RIP. Its convergence time is much faster. OSPF is not limited to routing across networks with 15 or fewer hops, and it takes into account the speed of a link in calculating routing tables. For these reasons, it has replaced RIP as the protocol most used by Internet routers.

OSPF is a link-state protocol. Link-state protocols assign a weight to each link. The criteria for computing weights is flexible, allowing the network administrator to take into account factors such as bandwidth, delay (e.g., satellite links have high bandwidth, but high delay), the number of networks crossed, the load, etc.

Link-state protocols have a reputation for complexity, which is OSPFs biggest disadvantage. OSPF can, however, be easily comprehended once its basic principles are understood.

Link-state protocols begin by introducing themselves to their neighbor. OSPF routers introduce themselves by transmitting "Hello" packets to any router with which it shares a common link. At the end of this stage, each router has in its table the unique IP addresses of the neighboring routers, and a description of the common link.

The next stage is for each router to advertise what it has learned from the Hello packets. This is done with a flooding technique. Each router transmits on each link a packet containing a list of its neighbors and the weight of the link. Each router that receives this packet transmits a copy on all available links, except the one on which it received it. This process results in each router quickly acquiring a complete link state database.

Potential clogging of the network caused by the flooding of link state advertisements is reduced in two ways: (1) if a router has previously received an advertisement, it is discarded, and (2) each packet is given a limited time to live, in terms of seconds, or hops.

As long as the network is operational, routers continue to introduce themselves to their neighbors by means of Hello packets. Typical Hello intervals range from 10 to 30 seconds. If a router fails to hear from one of its neighbors for two or three Hello intervals, or if it hears from a new neighbor, it advertises this fact by transmitting a packet containing the new information only. The new link state data is again advertised throughout the network by flooding. This process typically takes about one or two seconds.

The way routes are chosen on an OSPF network is left up to the individual router, but the algorithm that is used most frequently is Dijkastra's Algorithm. Fig. 4.5 can be thought of as nodes on a network with the integers representing the weight of the links. The algorithm works in the following way:

1. The starting node is made permanent and becomes the working node—in this case, node A as shown in Fig. 4.5(a).
2. Any node adjacent to the working node is labeled with the distance to the starting node and the node from which the probe was made (see Fig. 4.5(b)).
3. The node adjacent to the working node with the shortest distance to the starting node is made permanent.
4. If the node just made permanent is the destination node, then the shortest path has been found, else it becomes the new working node and step 2 is executed.

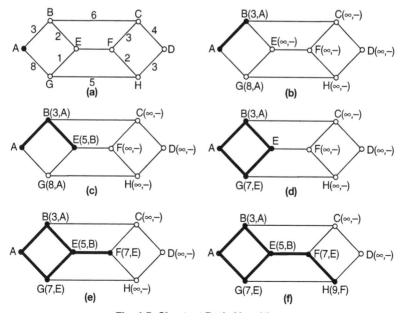

Fig. 4.5 Shortest Path Algorithm

One of the reasons that OSPF does not limit the number of hops, like RIP, is that OSPF networks are organized into smaller networks, referred to as autonomous systems, with still smaller networks within the autonomous system, referred to as area networks. *Gateways* are routers on the border of two networks. If a router selects a path to the correct gateway, the gateway will route the packet the rest of the way.

The organization of OSPF will be discussed in more detail in Chapter 7, The Internet.

Problem Solving Example:

Q What is the advantage of the OSPF routing protocol with respect to the RIP routing protocol? What is the advantage that RIP has over OSPF?

A The most important advantage of OSPF is that it takes into account the speed of the link when computing routing tables. Another, is that OSPF, unlike RIP, is not limited to fifteen hops. The advantage RIP has over OSPF is simplicity.

4.3 Factors Contributing to the Evolution of Network Layer Protocols

Complex networks, which utilize network layer protocols, have usually covered a wide geographic area. There are three reasons for this:

1. **Economics** - It is often too expensive to provide a direct link between every user node over a wide area (direct links are usually dedicated facilities provided by a public telephone company).

2. **Efficiency** - User nodes that are dispersed over a wide geographic area can communicate directly with a remote system by using the dial-up service of the public telephone network. However, for many applications, dial-up time contributes to unacceptably slow network operation. It is faster to route data through intermediate nodes connected by dedicated facilities.

3. **Reliability** - Reliability can be increased by a more complex network with intermediate nodes—if a link fails or is tempo-

rarily overloaded by network traffic, data can be routed through an alternate path.

There have been exceptions. Early local area networks sometimes routed messages through intermediate nodes. For example, the path control layer of IBM's SNA—the equivalent of the Reference Model's network layer—sometimes routes communication between local stations through intermediate nodes. Also, early computers separated by a wide geographic distance did not necessarily communicate through intermediate nodes. A good example is two large computers hundreds of miles apart directly linked by a dedicated facility such as a T1 line.

However, the primary impetus for the development of network layer protocols were economic and reliability factors that became increasing apparent as organizations transmitted computer data over farther and farther distances and between more and more remote end-stations. For example, IP was developed for a wide area network, the ARPANET.

One of first types of wide area networks were "packet switching networks." There are three kinds of wide area packet switching networks:

1. **Public -** These are referred to as public data networks (PDN) or public packet switching networks (PPSN). Public telephone companies provide packet switching services almost universally. One of the most common of these is the ITU-T X.25 standard.
2. **Private -** An organization may decide to build its own packet switching network. There are several manufacturers that will provide them with packet assemblers/disassemblers (PADs), switching nodes, and network controllers. Digital services offered by the public telephone network can be used for the network links. For example, DDS at 64 kbps can be used to connect the DCE device—the PAD—to a switching node, and high speed trunk lines, such as T1 lines, can be used to interconnect the switching nodes (see Fig. 4.6 on next page). When an organization employs dedicated facilities it is effectively building a private network within the public network.

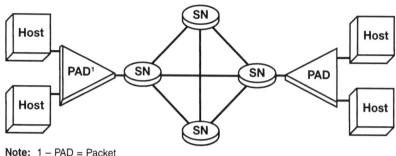

Fig. 4.6 Packet Switching Network

3. **Hybrid** - A private packet switching network can easily be integrated into a PPSN. In fact, most large switching networks are really hybrids, combining public and private transport services.

    Fig. 4.6 shows how a private packet switching network might be configured. The network links are what are called the "backbone" or the "backbone network," while the input lines to the PADs represent the access or the access network. Applications which justify a private facility are those which must support a high volume of data. Examples might include a bank or a financial institution.

    Applications which are suited for relying on a PPSN are low usage applications such as used in ATM machines or inquiries to corporate data bases.

    One of the fastest growing applications are interconnections between LANs. Data transmitted between LANs tends to burst and may not justify a dedicated link, especially over a long distance. This is because the cost of a dedicated link provided by the public telephone service is based on distance while the cost of data transmitted by a PPSN is based on volume.

    As telecommunications technology has evolved, interconnections between LANs has been increasingly relying on what are called *fast packet switching* networks. Fast packet switching technologies include *frame relay* and *asynchronous transfer mode* (ATM), both of which take advantage of lower error rates to minimize network level processing. Both frame relay and ATM will be discussed in Chapter 6. However, X.25 packet switching networks are still important and will be the subject of the next section.

4.3.1   The ITU-T X.25 Standard

The X.25 is a standard recommended by the ITU-T for packet switching public data networks. Although X.25 is often regarded as a network layer protocol, it actually defines three levels:

1. the Physical Level.
2. the Link Level.
3. the Packet Level.

The physical level of X.25 is defined by ITU-T recommended standards X.21 and X.21 bis, which define the electrical and mechanical characteristics of the physical interface. The X.21 standard was defined as an interface between DTE devices and digital DCE equipment. When the standard was first defined, most users wanted to interface with PDNs using modems, so X.21 bis (the French word for half) was defined as an interface between DTE devices and synchronous modems. X.21 bis is virtually identical to the EIA's RS-232-E. The bottom line is that any user whose DTE equipment has an RS-232-E interface is plug-compatible with X.25 DCE equipment.

The link level defined is the Link Access Procedure–Balanced (LAP-B), which is an ISO recommended standard. LAP-B is a subset of the class of procedures BAC, which was discussed in Section 3.2.1 on page 92.

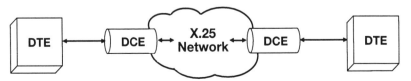

Fig. 4.7   DCE Interface to X.25 Network

The packet level of X.25 closely follows, but does not map directly into, the OSI Reference Model's network layer. Interestingly enough, X.25 is defined not as a network, but as an interface between a DTE device and a network, with a DCE device being right on the boundary between the equipment and the network, as shown in Fig. 4.7 on the previous page.

The standard says nothing about how packets are transmitted inside the network. Each inner network implementation can have its own link control, flow control, and network management. The network rout-

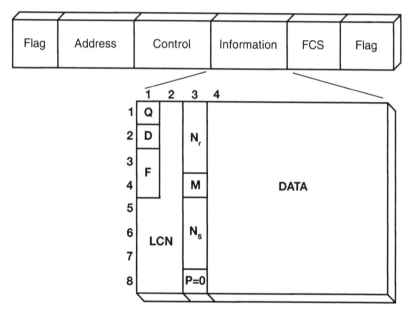

Fig. 4.8 X.25 Packet Contained in a LAP-B Frame

ing can be static or adaptive. However, the packet structure and the terminology make it clear that the service provided to the user is the sequential transmission of packets over a virtual circuit.

Fig. 4.8 shows the structure of an X.25 data packet within a LAP-B frame.

The fields of a data packet have the following significance:

1. **Q:** The qualifier bit allows a distinction to be made between data packets. This allows data packets to be transmitted on two flows.
2. **D:** Confirmation of delivery - If the D bit is 1, the network confirms delivery to network. If the D bit is 0, acknowledgments are end to end.
3. **F:** The format - If $F = 01$, the sequence numbers are modulo 8, if $F = 10$, the sequence numbers are modulo 128, and the header is four bytes. $F = 00$ or 11 applies to format of control packets.
4. **LCN:** Logical channel number - X.25 allows up to 4095 logical channels. LCNs have same significance as VCNs described in Section 4.1.3; also similarly the called DTE may be assigned a different LCN by the network.
5. **N_r:** Sequence number of packets received - This may be used for acknowledgment of data packets.
6. **M:** More data - If $M = 1$, more data packets will follow.
7. **N_s:** Sequence number of packets sent.
8. **P:** Packet type - If $P = 1$, it is a control packet with control information in the first seven bits of this byte in place of the sequence numbers and the more data bit.
9. **Data:** maximum length is assigned at time of subscription—most common is 128—may vary from 16 to 1024.

There are two kinds of X.25 connections:

1. **Permanent virtual circuit (PVC)** - This is the packet switching equivalent of a dedicated line. The logical channel number is assigned at the time of subscription.
2. **Virtual call (VC)** - This is basically the same thing as a virtual circuit, which has the same initials. A call is made by transmitting a setup packet, which contains the logical channel number and the address (in the data field). After the connection is made, succeeding packets' headers only require channel numbers.

Connections are made more quickly than a dial-up network, with connect-times of 100 ms typical. Packet data fields are short, on the order of 128 bytes, reflecting the philosophy that the packet can't be retransmitted at each node until the entire frame (which contains the packet) is received and processed at both the link and packet level. Currently, typical transmission speeds, from user nodes are 56 kbps with modems and DS1 (1.54 mbps) with digital DCE equipment.

The addresses that are transmitted with a setup packet are in accordance with the X.121 ITU-T standard, which specifies three fields: (1) a network identification code, (2) the country identification code, and (3) a terminal number.

Problem Solving Example:

 What is the economic advantage of access to a packet switching network, such as X.25, versus having a dedicated link?

With a packet switching network the organization is charged for total usage—the number of packets transferred. With a dedicated link the organization is not charged by usage, but by bandwidth allocated—whether it is used or not.

CHAPTER 5

Local Area Networks

A local area network (LAN) is defined as the hardware and software that provide the interface that allows computers distributed over a limited geographic area to communicate. In the 1980s there was an explosion in the number of local area networks with literally millions of new installations. This was actually the culmination of 25 years of technological development which included the PC and a myriad of other important advances.

The first local area networks borrowed heavily from technologies developed by the cable television industry. When Xerox Corporation began work in the 1970's on their Ethernet system, they relied upon high performance coaxial cable, transceivers, and connectors already being utilized by cable television systems.

However, the type of signalling techniques that LANs are designed to use are somewhat different from cable TV. Cable TV relies upon what is called "broadband" transmission to broadcast many analog channels on a single coaxial cable. Although some LANs utilize broadband transmission to accommodate two independent channels, most local area networks rely upon what is called "baseband" transmission. Baseband is a single channel transmission methodology, which can be analog, but in the case of LANs, digital baseband signalling is used.

In 1980 the IEEE 802 committee was formed to develop a standard for local area networks. Several of the organization's members wanted

Xerox's Ethernet to be accepted as the LAN standard. However, the IEEE committee agreed to look at several different implementations because other manufacturers were developing their own LAN technologies. Ethernet, with minor modifications, did end up being part of the 802 final draft as the 802.3 standard. Fig. 5.1 depicts the 802 final draft that was accepted by IEEE in December of 1982.

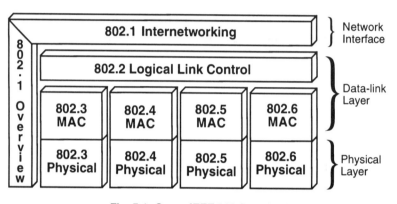

Fig. 5.1 Some IEEE 802 Standards

The 802.1 standard defines internetwork communication, network management, and an overview of how some of the different 802 standards fit together. There are two forms of internetwork communication described by 802.1: (1) medium access control (MAC) bridges which only require the services of the lower of the two data link sublayers—the MAC sublayer, and (2) the network layer interface as viewed from the data-link layer. Currently, for LAN applications requiring network layer services, the standard of choice is the TCP/IP protocol suite, which will be described in Chapter 7. In this chapter we will describe only MAC bridges.

The 802.2 standard defines the logical link control (LLC) sublayer of the data-link layer, as shown in Fig. 5.1. LLC is the same for all types of LANs.

The standards that vary from one type of LAN to another make up the MAC sublayer and the physical layer. They are defined by the following standards:

1. **802.3 standard:** Carrier sense multiple access/collision detection (CSMA/CD) LANs - This standard was based on Xerox's Ethernet and will covered in Section 5.2.
2. **802.4 standard:** Token Bus - This type of LAN is logically a token ring (see 802.5) but the physical topology is a serial bus.
3. **802.5 standard:** Token Ring - This standard was based on IBM's token ring and is the subject of Section 5.3.
4. **802.6 standard:** Metropolitan Area Networks (MANs) - MANs cover a wider geographic area than LANs and will be covered in Chapter 6 of this book.

After the IEEE 802 committee finished its initial work, in 1982, they submitted the LAN standards to the ISO. Eventually they were accepted by the ISO, with ISO standards 8802.1 through 8802.6 becoming the international equivalent to the IEEE's 802.1 through 802.6. The IEEE 802 recommendations were also accepted by the American National Standards Institute (ANSI) and are sometimes referred to as the IEEE/ANSI LAN standards.

5.1 Logical Link Control

The data-link layer of local area networks consists of two sublayers, with the higher sublayer being the logical link control (LLC). Fig. 5.2(b) on the next page shows a LLC protocol data unit. The LLC sublayer communicates with its peer on another network station by forming a PDU and passing it to the MAC sublayer, which encapsulates it into the information field of a MAC frame (see Fig. 5.2(a)), and then passes it to the physical layer in the form of a bit stream.

The control field of a LLC PDU is directly inspired by HDLC, as shown in Figs. 5.2(c)-5.2(e). The sequence number fields, N_s and N_r (see Fig. 5.2(c)), keep track of the number of LLC PDUs sent and received. The N_r field contains the sequence number of the next expected LLC PDU and can be used to acknowledge that LLC PDUs up to that sequence number were received without error.

The control field of supervisory and unnumbered LLC PDUs, as shown in Fig. 5.2(d) and Fig. 5.2(e), provide command and control

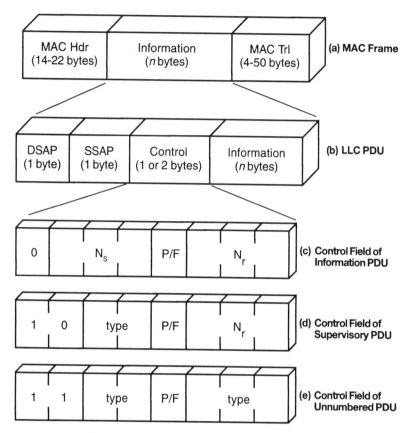

Fig. 5.2 Logical Link Control Protocol Data Unit

information in a way similar to HDLC described in Section 3.2 on page 92.

5.1.1 Classes of Procedure

There are two types of LLC procedure:

1. **Type 1:** A connectionless mode of operation - With this type of operation, LLC PDUs are transmitted as datagrams in what are called unnumbered information (UI) frames. There are no sequence numbers, acknowledgments, or commands. This type

of operation takes advantage of the low error rate of LANs. There may be a higher level that is responsible for error and flow control.

2. **Type 2:** A reliable connection-oriented mode of operation - A virtual circuit service is provided by the LLC sublayer, which includes sequencing, error, and flow control.

There are two LLC classes of procedure:

1. **Class 1:** provides Type 1 service only.
2. **Class 2:** provides both Type 1 and Type 2 service.

5.1.2   Logical Links

Service access points (SAP) provide the interface between the network layer and the LLC sublayer. Back and forth through these service access points are passed requests for service (from the network layer to the LLC), confirmations of services provided (from the LLC to the network layer), and (in both directions) information units.

The address fields shown in Fig. 5.2(a) contain the service access points. The destination service access point (DSAP) field contains the SAP of the destination station. The source service access point (SSAP) field contains the SAP of the source station. These SAPs allow the LLC to provide services for different application environments on the same station. For example, 06 is the SAP representing the internet protocol (IP).

These should not be confused with the physical addresses, which are added by the MAC sublayer along with other MAC fields, prior to transmission. The address fields of the LLC PDU provide "logical links" between different application environments, as shown in Fig. 5.3 on the next page.

The first bit of the DSAP address distinguishes between group addresses and individual addresses. In the SSAP address the first bit is used to distinguish between responses and commands. Of the 128 possible addresses, 64 are defined by the user and 64 are defined by the IEEE.

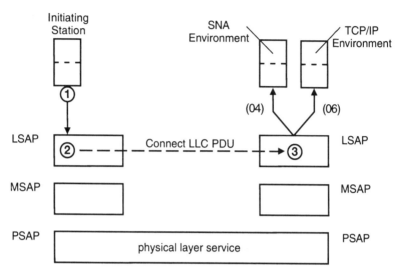

Fig. 5.3 Logical Link Addresses

5.1.3 Service Primitives

The IEEE LAN standards explicitly follow the OSI Reference Model. The LLC entities communicate with the network layer and with the MAC sublayer by the use of service primitives. Fig. 5.4(a) on the next page shows the L-CONNECT service primitive sequence and Fig.5.4(b) shows the L-CONNECT request parameters.

Primitives are an abstract way of describing inter-layer communication through service access points. The IEEE documents do not expressly define the implementation of primitives, but intuitively it is easiest to assume primitives are implemented by subroutine calls with parameters (see Fig. 5.4(b)). Fig. 5.4(c) shows additional primitives used to communicate between the network layer and the LLC sublayer. The difference between the L-DATA and L-DATA-CONNECT primitives is that the latter assumes that a connection has been established and the former does not.

The local-address and remote-address parameters, shown in Fig. 5.4(b), are the concatenation of the logical link addresses and the actual physical addresses. The logical link addresses are extracted to form

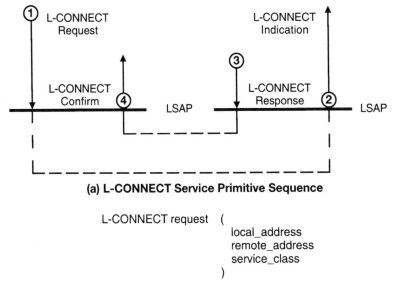

(a) L-CONNECT Service Primitive Sequence

L-CONNECT request (
       local_address
       remote_address
       service_class
)

(b) LLC Connect Request Parameters

Primitive	Type of Operation
L-DATA	Type 1
L-DATA-CONNECT	Type 2
L-DISCONNECT	Type 2
L-RESET	Type 2

Type 1 = Connectionless

Type 2 = Connection-oriented

(c) Primitive Operation Types

Fig. 5.4 LLC Service Primitives

the address fields of the LLC PDU (see Fig. 5.3 on previous page), while the physical addresses are passed to the MAC sublayer as parameters of the MA-DATA primitive, as shown in Fig. 5.5.

MA-DATA. request (
       destination_address
       m_sdu
       request_service_class
)

Fig. 5.5 MAC Data Request Primitive

The m_sdu parameter shown in Fig. 5.5 is the LLC PDU, which the MAC sublayer subsequently encapsulates into a MAC frame.

There is an inference in the above LLC discussion that could possibility be misleading. Although the LLC is defined by the IEEE 802.2 standard to communicate with the network layer though primitives depicted in Fig. 5.4, often local area networks have no need for network layer capability. Thus, in many cases, all the network layer does is pass information back and forth between the LLC and the transport layer.

5.2   Shared Media LANs

The IEEE 802.3 standard defines the medium access control (MAC) sublayer of the data-link layer and the physical layer for carrier sense multiple access/collision detection (CSMA/CD) LANs (see Fig. 5.1). These are also known as contention bus or shared bus LANs for the reason that stations will sometimes try to transmit simultaneously, or "contend" for, access to the physical medium.

These types of networks are based on a serial bus topology (see Fig. 1.9 on page 18). For a long time the majority of implementations in place relied on coaxial cable for physical support, however the most common physical support in use now is twisted pair cabling. There are also a few based on optical fiber. These physical configurations are most often used:

1. shielded coaxial cable (see Fig. 2.14 on page 74) of the thick Ethernet type. The characteristic impedance is 50 ohms. The length of a "segment" may be up to 500 meters with segments connected by repeaters allowing a total length of 2500 meters. The bit rate is 10 mbps with baseband signalling used. This type of LAN is based on the Ethernet *de facto* standard and is defined by the ISO 8802.3 10Base5 standard.
2. the thin Ethernet type of cabling (unshielded coax). Segments are limited to 200 meters (10Base2).
3. shielded 75 ohm coaxial cable. This configuration allows two signalling channels operated with broadband transmission (10Broad36).

4. unshielded twisted pair connected in a star configuration to a small coaxial bus at the hub of the LAN. This is the 802.3(i) standard (10Base-T) and the 802.3(u) Standard (100Base-T).
5. optical fiber. These types of LANs operate with an LED light source at a wavelength of 1300 nm. The optical fiber type is 125/62.5 (10Base-F/100 Base-FX) (see Fig. 2.15 on page 76).

Digital Encoding

Most types of shared bus networks utilize baseband signalling, using Manchester code as depicted in Fig. 2.13(c). This type of digital encoding requires as many as two transitions for each bit resulting in a bandwidth requirement that is double the bit rate. For example, a 10Base5 shared bus transmits with a bit rate of 10 mbps, and thus requires physical support capable of 20 Mhz. This is an efficiency of 50 percent. This is more than compensated by the ease of synchronization that is the result of a mandatory transition for every bit.

5.2.1   IEEE 802.3 Medium Access Protocol

The 802.3 standard provides for the CSMA/CD medium access protocol. Stations are allowed to transmit any time they do not "sense" a "carrier" on the bus. Collisions are "detected" by measuring the voltage level—if it reaches double the maximum level for a single carrier, then a collision is assumed. The minimum length for a MAC frame is 64 bytes, or 512 bits. Thus, with a bit rate of 10 mbps, the minimum frame can be transmitted in 51.2 µs. This is called the "slot time."

A 10Base5 bus (max. of 2500 meters with repeaters) can propagate a minimum frame from one end of the bus to another, allowing for delay caused by repeaters, in 48 µs. Another 3.2 µs is required to detect a collision. Thus, any station can detect a collision before the transmission of a minimum frame has been completed. If a collision is detected, the following recovery mechanism is in effect:

1. Both stations select a random number i ($0 \leq i < 2^k$) where k is the number of unsuccessful transmission attempts and where i is independently selected by each station.

2. Both stations wait a time iT to retransmit, where T is the slot time.

3. Each time there is an unsuccessful transmission, k is incremented, until it reaches a maximum value of 10, so that ($i \leq 1024$).

4. After 16 unsuccessful attempts, both stations give up.

The efficiency of a shared bus depends on how busy the network is. The busier it is the more time is spent resolving bus contention. Generally this type of LAN operates with an efficiency of around 95 percent.

Problem Solving Example:

Q What is the significance of the "slot time" on a shared bus LAN. In the event of a collision, why must a station wait at least one slot time before retransmitting?

A IEEE 802.3 MAC frames have a minimum length of 64 bytes, or 512 bits. This minimum frame can be transmitted, at a bit rate of 10 mbps, in 51.2 μs. This is called the "slot time."

It takes 48 μs for a minimum frame to propagate the length of a 10Base5 bus (max. of 2500 meters with repeaters), allowing for delay caused by repeaters. Another 3.2 μs is required to detect a collision. If a station waits one slot time before attempting to retransmit, it knows that all other stations have detected the collision, and those wanting to retransmit are implementing the CSMA/CD algorithm—i.e., waiting random multiples of a slot time, before retrying.

5.2.2 The 802.3 MAC Frame

Fig. 5.6 shows an 802.3 MAC frame.

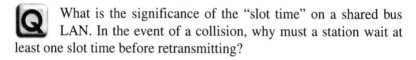

Pr	SFD	DA	SA	DL	Data	Pd	FCS
(7 bytes)	(1 byte)	(2 or 6 bytes)	(2 or 6 bytes)	(2 bytes)	(0-1500 bytes)	(0-46 bytes)	(4 bytes)

Fig. 5.6 802.3 MAC Frame

The fields of an 802.3 MAC frame have the following significance:

1. **Pr:** Preamble - used for synchronization. This field consists of seven bytes of alternating zeros and ones.
2. **SFD:** Starting frame delimiter - SFD = 10101011.
3. **DA:** Destination address - usually six bytes. If the first bit is 1, then it is a group address, else it is an individual address. If the second bit is 0, then it is a universal address assigned by the IEEE, else the address only has significance with the LAN.
4. **SA:** Source address - Same significance and size as the destination address.
5. **DL:** Data length - The number of bytes in the data field. This field contains the LLC PDU.
6. **Data:** The data field has a maximum frame size of 1500 bytes.
7. **Pd:** Padding - this field is only used to insure the minimum frame size of 64 bytes.
8. **FCS:** Frame check sequence - this field contains a 32 bit CRC used for error checking in a manner similar to that described in Section 3.1.

There are minor differences between the IEEE 802.3 standard and Ethernet, although the two terms are used almost interchangeably when referring to shared media LANs. The preamble of an Ethernet MAC frame is eight bytes, with no SD field (see Fig. 5.6 on previous page). Also, the DL field is used for two purposes: (1) to identify the protocol type, and (2) to provide the length of the data field.

5.2.3 Communication With Physical Layer

For communication between the MAC sublayer and the physical layer, the IEEE 802.3 standard provides for service primitives, as shown in Table 5.1 on the next page.

The PLS-DATA request primitive transfers frames to the physical layer in the form of a bit stream. The PLS-DATA indication primitive transfers frames to the peer MAC sublayer—also as a bit stream. The other primitives are used to gain access to the medium and to resolve bus contention.

Primitive	Communication Service
PLS-DATA	Peer to Peer
PLS-CARRIER	Interlayer
PLS-SIGNAL	Interlayer

Table 5.1 Physical Layer Service Primitives

5.3 Token Ring LANs

The IEEE 802.5 standard defines the medium access control (MAC) sublayer of the data-link layer and the physical layer for token rings (see Fig. 5.1). This standard, with a few minor modifications, is similar to IBM's token ring.

This type of network is based on a ring or loop topology (see Fig. 1.10 on page 19). Unlike the shared bus, which is built around a passive bus, a token ring network requires active connectors. This is because each station is responsible for relaying the *token* or frame to the next station; thus if one station goes down the whole network is unable to operate. Reliability of token ring networks is greatly enhanced by the use of concentrators as shown in Fig. 5.7 on the next page.

Several stations may be connected to a concentrator, which is capable of isolating a station, by switching relays, if it goes off-line. Also, if a second or alternate ring is available, the concentrator can, in the case of a break, reconfigure the ring by switching a relay (see Fig. 5.7).

The physical support provided for this type of network is usually shielded or unshielded twisted pair cables similar to those described in Section 2.6.1 on page 73. Twisted pairs have these advantages: (1) new stations can easily be added to the ring by plugging in RJ-45 modular jacks similar to phone jacks, (2) relatively low cost, and (3) flexibility and light weight. Data rates are usually 4 mbps with unshielded cables and 16 mbps with shielded cables.

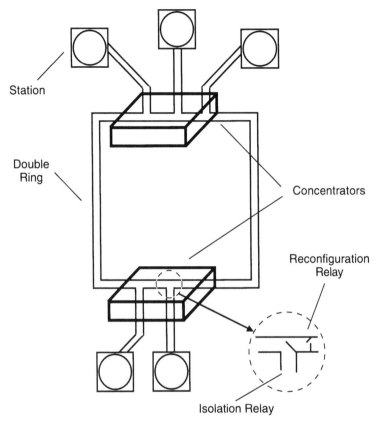

Fig. 5.7 Token Ring Concentrators

The type of digital encoding used is Manchester differential code which represents a 0 bit by the same configuration which preceded it and a 1 bit by the inverse configuration. Also included are special J and K symbols, which depart from conventional Manchester differential code, as shown in Fig. 5.8.

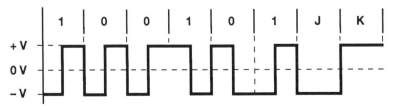

Fig. 5.8 Modified Manchester Differential Code

5.3.1　The 802.5 Medium Access Protocol

When a 802.5 token ring is not busy, it circulates a special frame called a token, with each station on the loop relaying the token to the next station. It could be said that a station may not transmit unless it has the token. However, that it somewhat of an oversimplification. In effect, as the token frame passes through the station that wants to send a message, it is converted and expanded to a data frame; the station changes the token bit to a 1, and inserts the following: the source and destination addresses, routing information (if required), its message in the data field, and a CRC polynomial for error checking.

When the destination station receives the data frame, it copies it. When the frame gets back to the source station, if it doesn't want to send another message, it changes the token bit back to a 0, and removes the fields it added.

5.3.2　The 802.5 MAC Frame

Fig. 5.9(a) shows a 802.5 MAC frame and Fig. 5.9(b) depicts the access control field. The token is a MAC frame minus the additional fields that are added when a station transmits a message (see Fig. 5.9(c)).

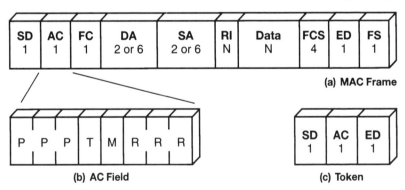

(a) MAC Frame

(b) AC Field

(c) Token

Fig. 5.9　Structure of a 802.5 Frame

The fields of a 802.5 MAC frame have the following significance:

1. **SD:** Starting delimiter - The SD field has the configuration JK0JK000.

2. **AC:** Access Control - The bits of the AC field (see Fig. 5.9(b)) have the following significance:
   - **PPP:** Priority - A station may only transmit if its priority level ≥ PPP.
   - **T:** Token - T = 0 indicates token frame. T = 1 indicates data frame.
   - **M:** set to 1 by transmitting station - When it passes through the monitor station, the monitor changes it to 0. If it is already 0 the monitor assumes the token or data frame has made more than one circuit of the ring. The monitor then purges the frame and transmits a new token, with the priority equal to 0, which is allowed to circulate continuously.
   - **RRR:** Reservation - If the current station has an authorized priority ≥ RRR, it may reserve the next token by storing the required priority in this field. However, a downstream station may still reserve the next token for a higher priority.
3. **FC:** Frame Control - This field enables data frames to be distinguished from ring management frames.
4. **DA:** Destination Address - Usually six bytes, this has the same significance as the DA field of a shared bus MAC frame.
5. **SA:** Source Address - Usually six bytes, this has the same significance as the SA field of a shared bus MAC frame.
6. **RI:** Routing Information - This field is optional and is only present if a frame must follow a path of more than one ring.
7. **Data:** This field does not have an upper limit, but it is limited by the retention time of the token, which is typically about 10 ms.
8. **FCS:** Frame Check Sequence - This field contains a 32-bit CRC polynomial.
9. **ED:** Ending Delimiter - This field contains JKJK1IE. The I bit indicates that this is an intermediate frame, with more data to come. The E bit indicates that some kind of frame error has been detected.
10. **FS:** Frame Status - This field indicates if the destination address was recognized and if the data was copied.

5.3.3 Monitor Station Responsibilities

In addition to purging bad tokens or frames from the ring, the monitor is also responsible for insuring that the ring latency, the time it take for the token to circulate, is greater than 24 bits—the length of the token.

The monitor is also responsible for resynchronizing the clock. Each station synchronizes its own clock with the SD field and maintains synchronization by means of the Manchester differential code, which requires one transition per bit. The way this works is: the station stores at least one bit element, and then retransmits it in synch with the incoming bit (or clock) transition. However, it is the monitor station's responsibility to eliminate accumulated clock imperfections by resynchronizing transmission with its own internal clock when it retransmits a token or frame.

The monitor periodically transmits an "active monitor present" frame. If there is no monitor present, a special claim token circulates on the ring with the station with the highest address eventually becoming the monitor.

Problem Solving Example:

Q Shared bus LANs and Token Rings have completely different topologies and operate with different protocols at the MAC sublayer. However, there are overriding concepts that both have in common which make both well suited for local area networks. What are those concepts?

A With both types of LAN topologies there is only one path between any two stations. This allows shared bus LANs and Token Rings to operate with a simple two-layered architecture: the physical layer and the data-link layer.

In the case of IEEE 802 LANs the upper data-link sublayer is logical link control (LLC). With shared bus LANs, the 802.3 MAC provides the LLC with CSMA/CD access to the physical link. In the case of Token Rings, the 802.5 MAC manages the store and forward operation of the ring, providing a "logical link" for the LLC.

Also, both of these types of networks avoid a mesh type of topology, which would result in the increased expense of providing substantially more physical connections.

5.4 MAC Bridges

The IEEE 802.1(d) standard defines "transparent bridges" that are used mostly to interconnect CSMA/CD LANs. Repeaters can be used to connect CSMA/CD shared bus segments; however, a repeater is a signal amplifier which transmits all traffic between segments. Bridges, on the other hand, operate at the MAC sublayer level, allowing them to analyze the destination address before propagating required frames to the interconnected network.

MAC bridges have two or more ports, each being connected to a different network. They are transparent in the sense that although each port has an address, the stations on the network do not transmit to the ports, but only include the addresses of the source and destination stations in their MAC frames. However, for several CSMA/CD LANs to be transparently transformed into a single larger network, each station on the interconnected network including bridge ports, must have a unique address.

The bridges learn about the interconnected network by monitoring LAN traffic. They maintain a table of the SA fields and the receiving port of each frame. If a bridge has not received a frame from a station for a specified time-out interval, the station is deleted from the table. When a bridge receives a frame one of three things can happen:

1. If it finds the frame originated on its own network, it does not retransmit the frame.
2. The bridge checks its table of associated SA fields and ports. If it finds the DA of the just received frame matches one of the earlier received SA fields in the table, it transmits the frame on the port associated with that SA field.
3. If the destination address is unknown, it transmits the frame on all ports except the one on which it received it.

This algorithm has a snag in the sense that unknown frames can keep looping indefinitely. For the sake of simplicity, in describing the solution to this problem, we will at first assume that each bridge has only two ports.

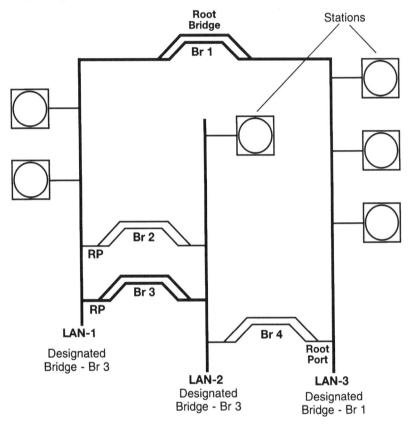

Fig. 5.10 Spanning Tree

The exchange of bridge protocol data units (BPDUs) is used to construct a "spanning tree" to prevent looping. The bridges with the lowest BPDU identifier is designated the "root bridge." Once the root is known each of the rest of the bridges designate a root port, to receive BPDUs. The root port is the port with the shortest distance (lowest path cost) to the root bridge. Also, BPDUs are used to select a designated bridge between each interconnected segment—the bridge with the lowest path cost to the root bridge. The distance to the root bridge is found by bridges forwarding BPDUs and adding to the path cost each time, with the resulting path cost analyzed by the forwarding bridges.

The bridges not chosen as designated bridges become blocked. The result is a tree structure which allows a frame to appear only once in each segment (see Fig. 5.10 on previous page).

The bridges that are blocked may still receive BDPUs in order that the spanning tree may be reconfigured in response to a change in network topology.

If bridges with more than one port are used, which is usually the case, a designated port is chosen for each segment, with the other ports being blocked—and the same principle applies. The most important thing is that there should be only one path from the root bridge to any segment, with no loops.

5.5   Twisted Pair Ethernet

Ethernet technology, developed by Xerox in the early 1970s, has lasted a surprisingly long time. A slightly different version of Ethernet was defined as the IEEE 802.3 Standard in the early 1980s. Although Ethernet is somewhat different from the IEEE 802.3 standard, it is common to use the term Ethernet to refer to both.

Ethernet has evolved considerably since the late 1980s. The original .75 Ohm coaxial cable, used for 10Base5 LANs, was thick, inflexible, and expensive to install. Soon, the less expensive 10Base2 Ethernet LANs, which use thinner cable and are limited to segments of 200 meters, became more popular. These so-called "thin-net" LANs use the same coax and connectors as cable television networks. The thinner coax is more flexible, less expensive, and new devices can be easily attached by "T-connectors" (see Fig. 5.11 on next page).

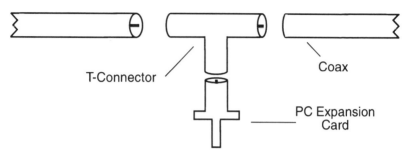

Fig. 5.11 T-Connector

However, the thin Ethernet cable has to be snaked to every computer. This led to the next stage in the evolution of Ethernet, the 10Base-T. The 10Base-T collapsed the shared bus down to a hub—where coaxial cable is still used. This allowed computers to be connected to the hub by twisted pairs. The unshielded twisted pairs are light, flexible, and very inexpensive. Encouraged by vendors, the IEEE, in a mere 18 months, standardized the 10Base-T as the IEEE 802.3(i). Soon, the 10Base-T became the most popular type of Ethernet (see Fig. 5.12)

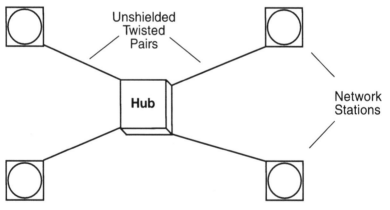

Fig. 5.12 10Base-T Configuration

In the 90's evolutionary forces have continued. The popularity of client-server architecture has resulted in network applications becoming more distributed, thus requiring more network communication. More powerful PCs and workstations, capable of a 100 million instructions per second (mips), have also been generating more network traffic. As shared bus collisions become more frequent, efficiency declines. One solution has been the development of *switched-Ethernet:* the hub becomes a fabric of interconnected switches which allow any two non-busy stations to communicate. In other words, rather than sharing the 10 mbps bus with 50, or 100, or more, other stations, each station basically gets full use of the 10 mbps bandwidth.

Switched-Ethernet stations are connected to the hub using unshielded twisted pairs, in the same star configuration as the 10Base-T shown in Fig. 5.12. Also, the CSMA/CD algorithm is preserved. In other words, the upgrade from 10Base-T to switched-Ethernet only requires replacing the hub.

Engineers have developed technology that allows 100 mbps transmission over unshielded twisted pairs. As a result, there is now a 100Base-T Ethernet, standardized as the IEEE 802.3(u). The 100Base-T retains the same star configuration, the CSMA/CD algorithm. 100Base-T is more expensive and distances are limited to 100 meters.

There is also the 100VG-AnyLAN, standardized as the IEEE 802.12. The VG refers to voice grade twisted pairs. The CSMA/CD algorithm is not retained, but it does support differing frame types, allowing a subset of stations to become a token ring. The Ethernet-based algorithm is replaced by a demand priority. Each station is polled, with access granted based on a simple priority. Distances for this LAN are also limited to 100 meters.

Problem Solving Example:

Why have Ethernet LANs gravitated toward a hub-based con figuration?

For economic reasons. A hub-based design allows the use of inexpensive, easy-to-install, unshielded twisted pair cables.

5.5.1   Attachment Unit Interface (AUI)

The attachment unit interface (AUI) was originally a way to connect NICs (installed in desktop computers) to transceivers physically adjacent to thick coaxial cable. Because that type of coax is unwieldy, there often was a significant distance between the cable and the computers. This distance, plus the fact that the transceiver's electronics require close proximity to the cable, resulted in the AUI having a maximum length of 50 m. Fig. 5.13 depicts the Ethernet controller architecture (the NIC), the architecture of the transceiver, and the AUI's connector and cable.

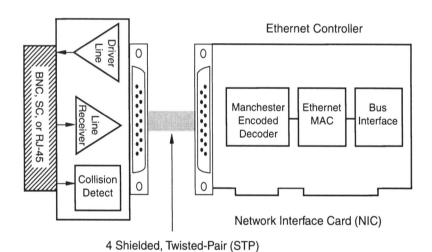

4 Shielded, Twisted-Pair (STP)
50 feet max.

Fig. 5.13 Architecture of Controller, Transceiver, and AUI Interface

The AUI, in the long run, became the accepted medium independent interface for 10 mbps Ethernets. The AUI is used with three types of connectors: (1) BNC with coaxial cable, (2) RJ-45 jacks with twisted pairs, and (3) SC with optical fiber. However, the AUI has been used mostly with 10BASE-T networks.

5.5.2 Medium Independent Interface (MII)

The medium independent interface (MII) was designed with the encoder/decoder as part of the transceiver. This is because the MII was intended to provide an interface for both 10 mbps and 100 mbps Ethernet devices, which operate with a variety of encoding schemes and signaling methods. Table 5.2 lists the types of 10/100 mbps Ethernets, their coding method, type of media, and the medium independent interface supported.

Ethernet Type	Data Coding	Line Coding	Physical Medium	Interface Type
10BASE5 *		Manchester	Coax.	AUI
10BASE2 *		Manchester	Thin Coax.	AUI
10BASE-T		Manchester	UTP 3/4/5 [1]	AUI, MII
10BASE-FL		Diff-NRZ	62.5 μm Op. Fiber	
100BASE-FX	4B/5B	NRZ	62.5 μm Op. Fiber	MII
100BASE-TX	4B/5B	NRZ	UTP 3/4/5	MII
100BASE-T2 *		PAM	UTP 3/4/5	MII
100BASE-T4	8B/6B	NRZ	UTP 3/4/5	MII

* Does not support auto-negotiation
[1] Refers to Category 3, 4, and 5 unshielded twisted pairs (UTP)

Table 5.2 10/100 mbps Ethernet Types

The MII has a much shorter cable than the AUI; the maximum length of its cable is defined as 0.5 m. It is intended to be used in a pigtail configuration, with the medium dependent connector (e.g. RJ-45 jack) attached to the other side of the transceiver. Fig. 5.14 (on the next page) shows the MII configuration and the architecture of the Ethernet controller (NIC) and the transceiver.

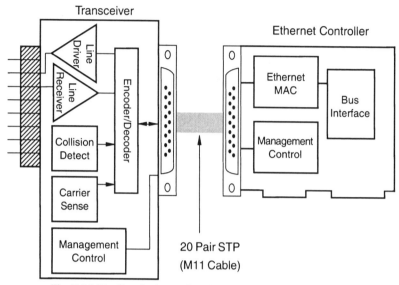

Fig. 5.14 Medium Independent Interface (M11) Architecture

The MII is similar to the AUI in that both are medium indepen-dent. But, unlike the AUI, the MII works with different data rates and coding methods. This can be convenient, but can also lead to prob-lems, because the MII makes it too easy to connect devices that are not configured to work with each other. For example, suppose one end of a UTP cable is attached to a wall plate and that a technician connects the other end to a desktop PC (using an RJ-45 jack). Since the end of the UTP that goes into the wall would probably be connected to a switch-ing hub, the likely result of this scenario would be a 10 mbps device (the desktop PC) being connected to a 100 mbps device (the switching hub). The technician could manually configure the switching hub to transmit at 10 mbps, but the hub would be located in a wiring closet—down the hall. And the wiring closet would probably be locked. The solution to this problem, and related incompatibility problems, is a tech-nique called auto-negotiation. Auto-negotiation will be covered in Sec-tion 5.5.4, following a discussion of flow control.

Unlike the AUI, which is a serial interface, the MMI provides a nibble wide data path between the controller and the transceiver. This enables the MII to be supported by a clock rate one fourth the bit rate. If the clock rate is 2.5 mHz, the bit rate is 10 mbps; if the clock rate is 25 mHz, the bit rate is 100 mbps.

5.5.3 Flow Control

A LAN switch is a multi-port bridge. Like a bridge, a switch operates at the level of the MAC sublayer. When a switch receives a frame on a particular port, it checks if the source address appears in the address table for that port; if it does not, the source address is entered into the table. Next, the switch checks if the destination address is included in the table. If it is, the frame is discarded because it would have already been received. If the destination address does not appear in the table for that port, the switch checks the address tables of other ports. If the address is found, the frame is forwarded accordingly. If the frame's destination address is not found at all, the switch will do one of two things: 1. it will forward the frame on all ports except the port on which it was received, or 2. if one of the ports is connected to a backbone switch or to a router, it may *uplink* the frame on that port only—on the assumption the unknown frame's destination is probably on the backbone network (in the case of a backbone switch), or on the Internet (in the case of a router).

The following terminology is often used when discussing switch performance:

1. **filter rate:** The rate at which a switch makes the decision to either discard or to forward a frame.
2. **relay rate:** The rate frames are actually forwarded on the output ports.
3. **wire-speed:** If a switch can continuously receive minimum length frames on all input ports, while simultaneously filtering and relaying them, it is a wire-speed switch.
4. **non-blocking:** This term was originally used to describe a central office (CO) of a telephone network. In this context a nonblocking CO has the switching capacity to handle all possible calls, except those whose destination line is busy. In the con-

text of a LAN, non-blocking describes a switch that has sufficient capacity to handle all input traffic, as long as the output traffic is evenly distributed over time.

5. **undersubscribing the bandwidth:** This means the switch has the sufficient internal capacity, in terms of buffers, to handle an uneven traffic flow for a significant time period. A non-blocking switch will usually undersubscribe the bandwidth by about 2:1.

A switching hub makes possible a *microsegmented*, star-wired Ethernet. Network devices may be connected to a repeating hub by dedicated links, but they still share bandwidth. But when the hub is a switch, it is possible for there to be only two devices on a segment: the switching hub and the device at the end of the link. This situation is true microsegmentation.

However, even in this situation CSMA/CD still applies, because there are still two devices competing for access: the switch and the end-station. For CSMA/CD access to no longer be required there must be a two-way link, plus full-duplex operation. Some examples of Ethernet devices with full-duplex capability include 100BASE-T2 devices, which are connected by dual UTP cables, and 100BASE-FX devices, which are connected by cables with dual optical fibers.

Before the advent of switching hubs, the issue of flow control was resolved at architectural layers higher than the MAC. Since Ethernet is defined at the MAC sublayer, and below, flow control had nothing to do with Ethernet. However, when high port density bridges became common place, congestion, related to uneven traffic flows, became a problem. For example, if a switch is receiving frames on several ports which are intended for output on a single port, the input buffers will eventually fill, and frames will have to be discarded.

Network administrators and equipment vendors tried a number of ways to alleviate congestion while remaining within Ethernet. One solution was to install wire-speed, non-blocking switches, but even then, prolonged uneven traffic flow still resulted in frame loss.

Another strategy to alleviate congestion relies upon the CSMA/CD algorithm to control traffic. Access to half-duplex links is arbitrated by CSMA/CD, allowing a technique called *back pressure* to be used to prevent congestion. If a switching hub's buffers have filled to where it will have to start discarding frames, it can continuously transmit a carrier signal—creating "back pressure." This would prevent any transmission on the link, and the switching hub's buffers from overflowing. However, on a full-duplex link there is no CSMA/CD, so the technique of back pressure cannot be used.

To allow Ethernet devices to realize flow control, the IEEE 802.3x committee defined a new sublayer: The MAC Control sublayer. Architecturally, the MAC Control sublayer is situated between the LLC and the MAC sublayer. Functionally, it has the responsibility of carrying out the PAUSE operation. The PAUSE operation was initially defined so that either, or both, of the devices on a full-duplex link could send special PAUSE frames to the other—preventing the other from sending non-Control frames, for a specified time period. The significant aspects of a PAUSE frame are as follows:

1. The type field contains the identifier 0x8808, which has been reserved for Ethernet MAC Control.
2. The MAC Control opcode field contains 0x0001, which is the opcode for the PAUSE operation.
3. The first two bytes in the MAC Control parameters field contain the number of slot times to wait before resuming transmission. Or, if this field equals 0, then the device will resume immediately.
4. The destination address field contains 0180C2000001, which is a multicast address reserved for the PAUSE operation.
5. The size of a PAUSE frame, or any MAC Control frame, is 64 bytes (512 bits).

The format of a MAC Control frame is depicted in Fig. 5.15 (on the next page).

Pr	SFD	DA	SA	Type = 0X8808	MAC Opcode 0X0001	Pause * Time	FCS
7	1	6	6	2	2	44	4

* 2 bytes for PAUSE time

Fig. 5.15 Special MAC Control Pause Frame

Currently, the use of MAC Control frames is limited to flow control on full-duplex links; however, the 802.3x committee left the door open to extend the PAUSE function to links operating in half-duplex mode. Also, the MAC Control sublayer is intended to eventually include additional functions.

5.5.4 Auto-Negotiation

The MII provides a medium independent interface for Ethernet devices that operate with varying data rates and signalling methods, and also devices that may or may not possess flow control capability. Since this makes it easy to connect incompatible devices, it is a good idea for them to automatically configure to the highest set of capabilities.

Because the data rate and the signalling method are not known, a known signalling method with a known data rate (6 mbps) is used for auto-negotiation, as shown in Fig. 5.16.

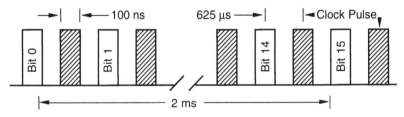

Fig. 5.16 Signaling for Auto-Negotiation

The auto-negotiation is carried out by exchanging 16-bit pages every 16 ms until the negotiation is complete. The 16-bit page is depicted in Fig. 5.17.

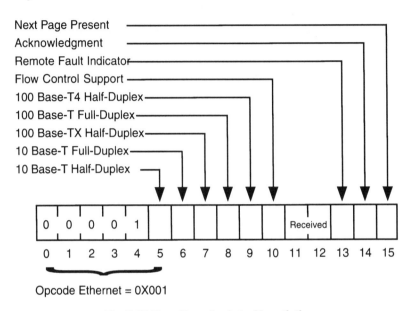

Opcode Ethernet = 0X001

Fig. 5.17 Base Page for Auto-Negotiation

CHAPTER 6

High Speed Networks

LANs have achieved fairly high transmission rates, from about 10 mbps to 100 mbps, and even up to 1000 mbps on LANs covered in this chapter. WANs, on the other hand, have tended to lag behind. The access rates to packet switched networks such as X.25, are for the most part limited to 64 kbps, and although access at the rate of a T1 line is expected to become widely available, even that may be too slow, because of exponential increases in the amount of data that will be transmitted across wide areas, and the expected need for rapid response times of future applications.

Organizations can connect two remote sites by the installation of dedicated facilities, such as multiples of DS-1. However, the flexibility that only a high-speed public packet switched network, or perhaps a high-speed hybrid of public and private facilities, is really what is needed.

6.1 Optical Fiber Networks

In the future, data communications will eventually be transformed by increased use of optical fiber, which is already being utilized for trunk lines by public telephone companies. In 1984, Bellcore Labs, the research arm of the regional Bell operating companies, submitted the first proposal for the Synchronous Optical Network (SONET). Table 6.1 (on the next page) shows the SONET hierarchy.

Sonet	Rate Mbps
STS - 1	51.84
STS - 3	155.52
STS - 9	466.56
STS - 12	622.08
STS - 18	933.12
STS - 24	1244.16
STS - 36	1866.24
STS - 48	2488.32

Table 6.1 SONET Hierarchy

SONET has defined a detailed standard that in a sense is similar to the North American Hierarchy. Both require frames to be transmitted every 125 µs to be compatible with the 125 µs sampling interval of 64 kbps voice channel. Both hierarchies consist of multiples of a basic service, 64 kbs DS0 for the North American Hierarchy, and 51.84 mbps STS-1 for SONET. However, SONET is very complex and beyond the scope of this book.

In this chapter we will examine leading edge technologies that are used to implement high speed networks—especially over wide areas.

6.1.1 Synchronous Optical Network (SONET)

SONET is the optical fiber equivalent of the T1 digital carrier system. Both a T1 multiplexer and a SONET terminal/service-adapter transmit a frame every 125 µs. The basic unit of the T1 carrier system is the DS-1 frame (193 bytes), while the basic unit of SONET is the STS-1 frame (8100 bytes). A DS-1 signal is converted to BPRZ-AMI code, and then placed on a specially treated copper pair—where it becomes a T1 carrier. The STS-1 signal is scrambled to prevent a long series of 0s or 1s, converted from an electrical to an NRZ-coded optical signal, and then transmitted on an optical fiber—where it becomes an OC-1 carrier.

Complexity of SONET vs. T1

SONET is more complicated than T1. This is primarily because SONET was designed to provide a compatible interface for several different types of traffic: 1. T1 carrier signals, DS-0 to DS-4, 2. The ITU-T hierarchy, 3. ATM, and 4. FDDI.

In addition, because one fiber carries so much traffic, a SONET network must be capable of recovering rapidly from a cable break or a node failure. Fig. 6.1 depicts a SONET backbone network. Note the varying kinds of data traffic, the self-healing mechanism, and the three types of network nodes: *terminal/service-adapters*, *add/drop multiplexers*, and *cross-connect switches*.

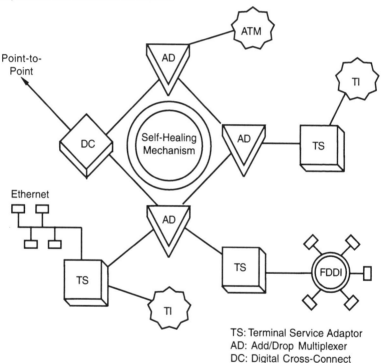

TS: Terminal Service Adaptor
AD: Add/Drop Multiplexer
DC: Digital Cross-Connect

Fig. 6.1 SONET Network

Because of the need for rapid recovery in the event of failure, the STS-N format includes what are called embedded operations channels (EOCs). The overhead of each frame includes two bytes, called K bytes, which contain switching protection information. Also, part of the STS-1 overhead, the D bytes, are used to carry messages such as the alarm indication signal (AIS), and the remote failure indication (RFI).

Another reason for the complexity of SONET vs. T1 is the need to economically access a small amount of data. The T1 carrier system demultiplexes an entire frame, reroutes the channels with separate destinations, then re-multiplexes the frame before retransmission. The SONET system relies upon add/drop multiplexers and a system of pointers, contained in H bytes, to add or drop a signal as small as a 64 kbps DS-0 channel while the frame stays intact.

Layers of the SONET System
The architecture of a SONET network is structured in four layers (see Fig. 6.2):

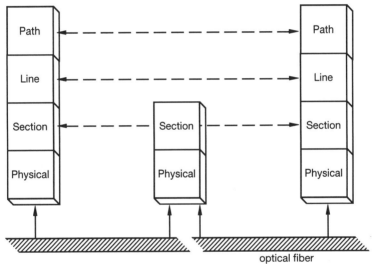

Fig. 6.2 SONET Architecture

1. **Path Layer:** Governs end-to-end communication. Typically the end-points of a *path* are terminal/service-adapters.
2. **Line Layer:** Responsible for multiplexing data onto, and dropping data from SONET frames. While the section layer creates the frame, the *line* layer inserts the data into the *synchronous payload envelope* (SPE). The line layer also handles protection switching and synchronization.
3. **Section Layer:** A section is a single run of optical fiber. The *section* layer creates and regenerates SONET frames. Usually at

least one of the endpoints of a section is a regenerating repeater.

4. **Physical Layer:** The physical layer is responsible for the transmission of an optical signal across the physical medium. (Technically, a SONET signal can also be electrical, although for only a limited distance, because of the high bit rates.)

The H1 and H2 bytes of the line overhead are usually viewed as one word. Bits 1-4 contain a new data flag which indicates a new pointer needs to be assigned in the SONET payload. When bits 1-4 contain 1001, a change has been signaled, while bits 1-4 = 0110 indicates normal operation.

The payload is allowed to float within the STS-1 SPE (occasionally slip back or advance one byte position because of minor differences between the SONET clock and the STS clock). That is why, in Fig. 6.3 on the next page, a good portion of the path overhead and the SONET payload overlaps onto the next STS-1 SPE. Also, in Fig. 6.3, a good portion of the previous payload is contained in the current STS-1 SPE.

Bits 7-16 of the H1 and H2 bytes contain a pointer to the first byte of the payload, the J1, or path trace byte. When the pointer equals 0, the J1 byte is adjacent to the H3 byte of the line overhead. When the pointer equals 782, its maximum, the J1 byte is in the last column of the last row of the SONET frame (see Fig. 6.3). When the payload slips back one byte position, the I-bits of the pointer (bits 7, 9, 11, 13, & 15) are inverted. When the I-bits have been inverted, this signals that the payload has just slipped back one byte.

At this point in time there would normally be a one byte gap between the end of the previous SONET payload and the beginning of current payload (the one normally pointed to by bits 7-16 of H1-H2). This one byte gap is dealt with by stuffing a byte in the first position following the H3 byte. Since the current payload (the one that just slipped back one position) becomes the previous payload of the next SPE, when the next frame arrives both the previous and current payload will have slipped back one position. This means everything will be lined up, and there will be no gap that requires stuffing. Therefore, the I-bits need no longer be inverted, allowing the pointer (to J1) to be incremented. When the payload advances one position relative to the STS-1 SPE, the situation is handled in a similar, but reverse manner. An additional space of one byte is created—to allow the payload to advance one byte position—by storing one byte in H3. Also, the D-bits (8, 10, 12, 14, & 16) are inverted. When the next frame arrives, every-thing will be lined up and the D-bits will no longer need to be inverted, allowing the pointer (to J1) to be decremented.

The SONET Frame

A STS-N frame has two main parts: the transport overhead and the synchronous payload envelope (SPE). The transport overhead consists of the section overhead and the line overhead. The SPE contains the path overhead.

A STS-1 frame (8100 bytes) is made up of nine rows of 90 col-umns each, as shown in Fig. 6.3. The transport overhead (27 bytes) is contained in the first three columns. The path overhead is located in the first 9-byte column of the SPE. Because the SPE is allowed to float, the location of the path overhead may vary.

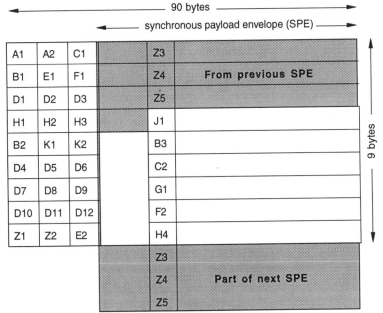

Fig. 6.3 STS-1 Frame

Studying the SONET frame structure for the first time may seem like trying to logically analyze a bowl of alphabet soup. Fortunately, most of the confusion can be avoided by being aware of the recurring patterns, similarities, and differences occurring among the three types of overhead. For example, the B_N bytes are included for parity checking in all three types of overhead. Also, the D_N bytes provide a data communication channel for both the section and line layer. Other similarities include: (1) the E_N bytes being utilized as a voice channel between section endpoints, and also line endpoints; (2) the F_N bytes being left as user defined in both the section and path overhead; (3) the use of the first non-framing byte of the section overhead, C1, for section trace, and the first byte in the path overhead, J1, for path trace; and (4) the Z_N bytes, which remain under study.

Part of the STS-1 overhead is for signal format, while a significant portion—the embedded operations channels (EOCs)—is utilized for operations and maintenance (OAM). An example of information used for signal format is the pointer to the path overhead contained in the H1, H2 bytes. Examples of EOCs include the K1, K2 bytes—alluded to earlier, which contain switching protection information, and the G1 byte, which contains path status information.

Table 6.2 provides a description of the path and line overhead. Note that an STS-N frame is formed by interleaving N STS-1 frames—for some types of overhead only the byte from the first STS-1 frame is utilized.

Section Overhead Bytes

A1, A2:   Framing bytes, A1 = F6, A2 = 28

C1:   Section trace. For an STS-N frame each C1 contains the STS-1 ID, from 1 to N.

B1: Bit interleave parity (BIP)[1]. Contains even parity for all corresponding bits over the previous STS-N.

E1: Orderwire[1]. Provides 64 kbps voice channel for section level communication between regenerators, hubs, and remote terminals.

F1: User channel[1]. Provides 64 kbps channel for user purposes.

[Table 6.2 continued on next page]

[Table 6.2 continued from previous page]

D1—D3: Data communications channel[1]. Provides 192 kbps channel for OAM at the section level.

[1] defined only for the first STS-1 of an STS-N.

Line Overhead Bytes

H1—H3:   Pointer bytes. Bits 7-16 of bytes H1-H2 point to the first byte of the SPE. Bits 1-4 of H1-H2 contain 1001 if the SPE has just been modified, else 0110. H3 is used for negative byte stuffing (see Section 5.2).

B2:   Bit interleave parity. Contains even parity for all corresponding bits over the line overhead and the previous STS-1 payload.

K1, K2:   Automatic protection switching channel[1].

D4—D12:   Data communications channel[1]. Provides 576 kbps channel for OAM at the line level.

E1:   Orderwire[1]. Provides 64 kbps voice channel between line terminating equipment.

Z1, Z2:   Reserved for future use.

[1] defined only for the first STS-1 of an STS-N.

Path Overhead Bytes

J1:   Path trace. Used to repetitively transmit a user definable 64-byte string to enable the continuous monitoring of the path's integrity.

B3:   Bit interleave parity. Contains even parity for all corresponding bits over the SPE.

C2:   Path signal label. Indicates construction of the SPE, such as: path connection, but no data sent (C2 = 0), non-specific SPE (C2 = 1), floating virtual tributary (VT) mode (C2 = 2), etc.

G2:   Path status. Used to convey the path terminal status and performance. The first four bits contain a count of the number of BIP errors. The fifth bit represents a remote defect indication (RDI).

H4:   Multiframe indicator. Used for payloads longer than one frame.

Z3—Z5:   Reserved for future use.

Table 6.2 STS-1 Frame Overhead

6.1.2   Fiber Distributed Data Interface (FDDI)

The ANSI X3D9.5 FDDI standard operates with a topology and protocol very similar to an IEEE 802.5 token ring. However, FDDI was defined to operate over a much wider geographic area and at much higher data rates. An FDDI network is characterized by:

1. Multimode graded index 125/62.5 optical fiber (see Fig. 2.15 on page 76) is most often chosen for the physical medium. The light source is usually an LED operating with a wavelength of 1300 nm (beyond 1300 nm requires laser diodes). Monomode fiber and twisted pairs can also be selected as physical support for this standard.
2. Distances between stations can vary up to 2 km with multimode fiber. If twisted pairs are used the separation is limited to 100 m.
3. The maximum number of stations is 500.
4. The total length of the network with multimode fiber and 500 stations is limited to 100 km. This assumes the network is operating with an alternate ring. If a cable break caused the network to recover by reconfiguring to a double loop the total length would reach 200 km.
5. A transmission rate of 100 mbps is most common.

NRZI 4B/5B Encoding

The "power budget" of an optical fiber link is the difference between the maximum power output of the light source and the minimum power required by the photo detector. With an LED source and a pho-

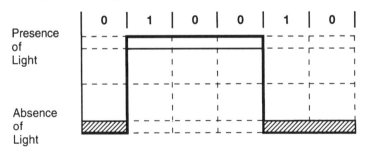

Fig. 6.4 NRZI Encoding Applied to Optical Fiber

todiode detector, the power budget is around 11 dB. Allowing for loss due to optical splices and connectors, the attenuation of a graded index multimode fiber at a distance of 2 km, and with a modulation rate of 125 mbaud, is 11 dB. Thus, the maximum modulation rate is 125 mbaud.

If Manchester code, which has an efficiency of 50%, were used, the maximum bit rate would be 62.5 mbps. To increase the capacity of the links the FDDI standard calls for a *non-return-to-zero inverted* (NRZI) 4B/5B encoding scheme. An example of NRZI encoding, which means ones are inverted and zeros result in no change, is shown in Fig. 6.4 on the previous page.

Symbol		Significance
Name	**Coding**	
I	1 1 1 1 1	Idle - padding
H	0 0 1 0 0	Halt
K	1 0 0 0 1	Frame Delimiter
R	0 0 1 1 1	Logic '0'
S	1 1 0 0 1	Logic '1'
0	1 1 1 1 0	Hex '0' - 0 0 0 0
1	0 1 0 0 1	Hex '1' - 0 0 0 1
2	1 0 1 0 0	Hex '2' - 0 0 1 0
3	1 0 1 0 1	Hex '3' - 0 0 1 1
4	0 1 0 1 0	Hex '4' - 0 1 0 0
5	0 1 0 1 1	Hex '5' - 0 1 0 1
6	0 1 1 1 0	Hex '6' - 0 1 1 0
7	0 1 1 1 1	Hex '7' - 0 1 1 1
8	1 0 0 1 0	Hex '8' - 1 0 0 0
9	1 0 0 1 1	Hex '9' - 1 0 0 1
A	1 0 1 1 0	Hex 'A' - 1 0 1 0
B	1 0 1 1 1	Hex 'B' - 1 0 1 1
C	1 1 0 1 0	Hex 'C' - 1 1 0 0
D	1 1 0 1 1	Hex 'D' - 1 1 0 1
E	1 1 1 0 0	Hex 'E' - 1 1 1 0
F	1 1 1 0 1	Hex 'F' - 1 1 1 1

Table 6.3 FDDI 4B/5B Symbols

With NRZI the transmission of a series of zeros can result in a loss of synchronization, because of the lack of a transition. For this reason,

4B/5B encoding was chosen. This type of encoding represents each four bits with a five-bit symbol. To insure sufficient transitions for synchronization, FDDI only uses symbols with at least two ones and no more than three consecutive zeros, as shown in Table 6.3 on the previous page.

NRZI 4B/5B encoding is 80% efficient allowing in a bit rate of 100 mbps with multimode optical fiber.

Synchronization

Unlike the token ring, an FDDI network does not have a monitor station provide a reference clock for synchronization. Due to the high data rate, the accumulation of inaccuracies make a single reference clock impractical. The solution of FDDI is for each station to have a flexible input buffer register of ten bits.

The input buffer is reset after each frame. This allows a variation of four and one half bits. With a frequency deviation of 10^{-4}, this allows a frame length of 45,000 bits or 9000 symbols. With five bits per symbol, this allows a frame length of 4500 bytes.

Architecture of FDDI

The ANSI X3D9.5 committee departed somewhat from the IEEE's approach when they defined the architecture of an FDDI network. FDDI is similar to the two networks that it is most often compared to—the DQDB MAN and the token ring LAN—in that it operates under the IEEE 802.2 LLC. However, the physical layer is divided into two sublayers, and station management functions are defined in a separate functional module, as shown in Fig. 6.5(a) on the next page.

The station management function (SMT) is responsible for the general functions of network management, such as ring initialization and recovery in case of a break in the medium or a station going down.

The upper physical sublayer, FDDI PHY, is responsible for medium independent functions such as encoding and synchronization (see Fig. 6.5(b)). The physical medium dependent (PMD) sublayer consists of the physical components that vary, depending on the implementation. Multimode fiber, monomode fiber, and twisted pairs each have a defined PMD which is a description of connectors, transducers, etc.

FDDI Frame Format

Fig. 6.6 on the next page shows an FDDI frame, which is very similar to a token ring frame described in Section 5.3 on page 130. The

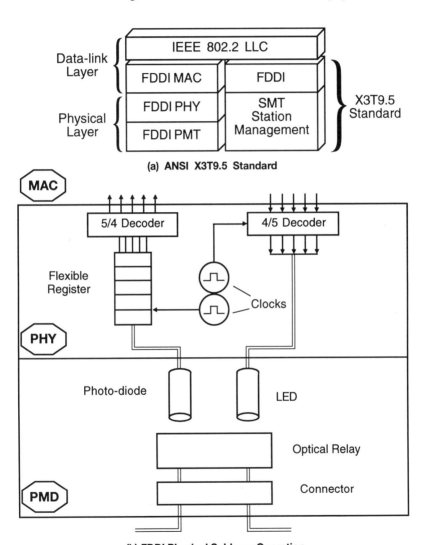

(a) **ANSI X3T9.5 Standard**

(b) **FDDI Physical Sublayer Operation**

Fig. 6.5 FDDI Architecture

numbers in the frame fields represent the number of symbols (two symbols for each byte—see Table 6.3).

The fields of an FDDI frame have nearly identical significance as the fields of a token ring frame. One difference is that a longer preamble is required for synchronization due to the high bit rate. Another difference is that one of the bits of the frame control field is used to indicate whether the transmission is synchronous or asynchronous (which will be explained later). Also, the number of bytes in the data field is limited to 4500 whereas the size of a token ring's data field is only limited by the retention time of the token.

FDDI Protocol

When the ring is initialized, what is called a MAC claim frame is circulated on the ring. The MAC claim frame is used to negotiate a target token rotation time (TTRT). When a station receives the claim frame, it replaces the existing TTRT if it requires a shorter TTRT, or it only retransmits the frame. Eventually the TTRT of the most demanding station is retained for ring operation.

When the ring is initialized, SMT frames are also used to allocate a portion of the "synchronous flow" to each station. For example, if the TTRT is 10 ms and the portion of the synchronous flow allocated to a particular station is 1 ms, then every 10 ms that station is guaranteed 1 ms of transmission time—called synchronous transmission.

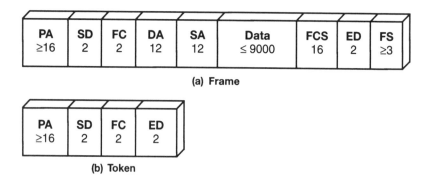

(a) Frame

(b) Token

Fig. 6.6 FDDI Frame

In addition to synchronous transmission, stations are allowed asynchronous transmission, if the token arrives early. For example, if the TTRT = 10 ms, but for a given rotation the (target rotation time) TRT = 7 ms, then the station in possession of the token is allowed 3 ms of asynchronous transmission in addition to its synchronous transmission.

6.1.3 FDDI-II

FDDI-II is an upwardly compatible extension of FDDI. It adds *circuit-switched data services* that can be used for isochronous applications such as voice, video, or image transfer.

Because voice or video can be garbled by even a short delay, stations requiring isochronous communication are guaranteed a portion of the frame's data field on every rotation. This is called circuit-switched data service. That part of a frame that is dedicated to circuit-switched data can be subdivided into "channels" which are allocated to stations transmitting voice (usually 64 kbps), or high quality video (usually 6.1 mbps).

FDDI, in its original form, is not very good at constant bit rate, isochronous transmission. FDDI has a synchronous traffic class, but even that does not guarantee a fixed delay, only a minimum bit rate.

FDDI-II can operate in basic mode—the equivalent of FDDI—or in hybrid mode. If it is operating in hybrid mode, a frame called a cycle is generated every 125 μs by a special station called a cycle master. Each cycle consists of a short preamble, followed by a 12 byte header, followed by a data field of 1548 bytes, for a total of 12,500 bits per cycle. The data rate is given by:

$$(12{,}500 \text{ bits/cycle}) / (125 * 10^{-6} \text{ s/cycle}) = 100 \text{ mbps}$$

The data field includes 16 *wideband channels* of 96 bytes. This allows a data rate of 6.144 mbps for each wideband channel.

There is also a dedicated packet group of 12 bytes, which provides a minimum data of 768 kbps. The dedicated packet group operates under LLC, and its PDUs are MAC frames. The dedicated packet group can be extended by adding wideband channels one at a time, for a maximum of 99.702 mbps, that can be used for regular FDDI traffic.

All 16 of the wideband channels can be used for isochronous virtual circuit transmission such as voice or video. The wideband channel can be subdivided, with the smallest subchannel being 1 bit, or 8 kbps. Stations can be allocated subchannels of 2^n bits per wideband channel, for $0 \leq n \leq 9$. If $n = 9$, then the full wideband channel of 6.144 mbps is allocated to the station.

If all of the wideband channels are allocated for circuit-switched data, the aggregate rate is 98.304 mbps for isochronous data. There are, of course, various possibilities in between. If the dedicated packet group was extended by adding three wideband channels, there would be 19.2 mbps available for MAC frames, and 79.104 mbps available for circuit-switched data.

The allocation of channels or subchannels for isochronous transmission is a station management function.

Problem Solving Example:

 Why did the American National Standards Institute (ANSI), define FDDI-II as an extension of FDDI?

There is no provision in FDDI for time-sensitive data such as audio or video. Even FDDI's synchronous traffic class only guarantees a minimum sustained data rate, not a fixed delay. FDDI-II allows stations to be allocated wideband channels, or portions of wideband channels, for virtual circuits that guarantee a fixed delay of 125 μs.

6.2   High Speed Local Area Networks

In the late 1990s, Ethernet emerged as the LAN of choice for high data rates. Ethernets have an advantage in that they are simple to operate. Ethernets do not require one of the stations to act as the network monitor; nor do Ethernet stations have to be concerned with such complexities as access priority.

The need for faster LANs is the result of two factors: (1) the more rapid data processing and transmitting capability of PCs, workstations, and servers; and (2) the proliferation of multi-level campus networks. In the mid 80s a VAX mini-computer could not saturate a 10 mbps network. In the late 90s powerful servers may require multiple 100 mbps connections, and campus backbone networks often operate in the gigabits-per-second range.

At the desktop level the most common LAN is still the 10BASE-T, although, in most cases, the network hub is now a switch rather than a repeater. As shown in Fig. 6.7, a switching hub allows micro-segmented half-/full-duplex links to operate at independent data rates. The switch-

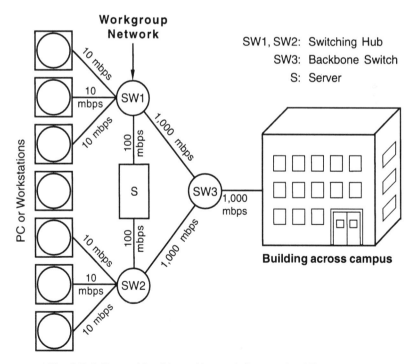

Fig. 6.7 Collapsed Backbone Network Connecting Workgroups

ing hub may also be connected to one or more servers—forming a *workgroup*. Several workgroup Ethernets may, in turn, be connected by 100/1000 mbps links to a high-performance switch—with the resulting configuration forming what is called a *collapsed backbone* network (see Fig. 6.7).

6.2.1 Structured Wiring

A hub is a device at the center of a star-wired network. A hub may be: (1) a repeater, which operates at the physical layer; (2) a switch, which operates at the level of the data-link layer; or (3) a router, which operates at the network level, providing TCP/IP connectivity. While a router may be connected to an Ethernet, it is not technically part of the Ethernet network because LANs operate strictly at the first two layers.

The connecting links between a workgroup's end-stations (desktop computers and servers) and its hub (usually a switch) are referred to as the Ethernet's *horizontal distribution*. The connecting links of an Ethernet's collapsed backbone network are referred to as its *vertical distribution*. In the early 90s the most common cable use for horizontal distribution was thin coax or 150 μm shielded twisted pairs (STP). Now the most common is Category 3 unshielded twisted pairs (UTP). Replacing thick coax as the most common cable for vertical distribution is 62.5 μm multimode fiber.

If UTPs are used, the maximum distance for horizontal distribution, including the distance from the wall plate to the desktop, is 100 m. Since this distance may extend in any direction from the hub, the maximum horizontal *extant* is 200 m. The maximum distance for vertical distribution is about 2 km, depending upon the type of media and the transmission technology.

The origins of standards for structured wiring date to the first digital PBX. Category 3 UTPs were first developed for use with digital PBXs, and was later standardized by the EIA/TIA. This initial work eventually led to the EIA/TIA 568 series of standards for structured wiring. The widespread acceptance of structured wiring meant: (1) hubs could conveniently be located in wire closets, (2) each work place could have a dedicated cable—from the wall plate to the desk, (3) network moves/adds/changes could be greatly facilitated by simply plugging/ unplugging RJ-45 connectors (an eight-wire equivalent of the RJ-11 telephone jack).

6.2.2 Redesigning the CSMA/CD for Gigabit Ethernet

One of the advantages of using switching hubs is that they make possible a microsegmented environment. Devices connected to a repeating hub have dedicated links, but they share *bandwidth*, and thus compete for access using CSMA/CD. A switching hub allows each station to inhabit a separate collision domain. In fact, if the link between a station and a switching hub is full-duplex, there is no possibility of collision. This means the use of the CSMA/CD algorithm can be dropped entirely.

The elimination of the need for the CSMA/CD algorithm on a full-duplex link has important implications. Without CSMA/CD it is not necessary for the farthest end-station to be able to detect collision during one slot time (the time it takes to transmit a minimum length frame). Therefore, full-duplex links are not restricted by a maximum length. This allows a full-duplex link to be extended to any distance—perhaps hundreds, or even thousands of miles, on a dedicated T1 line or SONET carrier.

On the other hand, the slot time is still an important parameter on Gigabit half-duplex links, because they require CSMA/CD to operate. The slot time on any Ethernet network is 512 bit times. On a 10 mbps Ethernet the slot time is 51.2 µs, on a 100 mbps Ethernet it is 5.12 µs, and on a Gigabit Ethernet it is only 512 ns. Unfortunately a slot time of this duration would mean the maximum length of a half-duplex Gigabit link would be less than 20 m.

One solution would be to operate all Gigabit links in full-duplex mode, then it wouldn't matter that the slot time is only 512 ns. However, repeating hubs operate with half-duplex links, and many switching hubs include half-duplex as an option. And both are part of the Gigabit Ethernet standard. The solution the standards developers came up with is to decouple the slot time from the minimum length frame. The minimum length frame for Gigabit Ethernet, as defined by Clause 2 of the IEEE 802.3z specification, is 4096 bytes. This represents the old 64 byte (512 bit) minimum frame plus a non-data carrier extension, as shown in Fig. 6.8. The net result is that at Gigabit rates any two stations on a 100 m link can detect a collision before a minimum length frame has completed transmission.

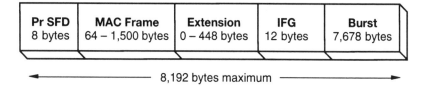

Pr SFD 8 bytes	MAC Frame 64 – 1,500 bytes	Extension 0 – 448 bytes	IFG 12 bytes	Burst 7,678 bytes

←──────────── 8,192 bytes maximum ────────────→

Fig. 6.8 Gigabit Frame Burst Including Extension (if needed)

The slot time on Gigabit Ethernets remains 512 bit times and is still used to compute the collision backoff time.

The change in the minimum length frame is transparent to higher layers, because the carrier extension is handled strictly at the data link level. This means that Gigabit Ethernet is backwards compatible with network drivers and application software.

Another change to the CSMA/CD algorithm is the addition of a mechanism called *frame bursting*, as shown in Fig. 6.8. The addition of carrier extension (non-data characters) introduces at least some inefficiency, and if the traffic on a particular network includes a lot of short frames, the loss of efficiency can be significant. Gigabit Ethernet minimizes this inefficiency by allowing stations to transmit frame bursts of up 8192 bytes. Since all of the frames, except the first one of a burst, do not require carrier extension, but only must conform to the more customary 512 bit minimum, at most 448 bytes of a 8192 byte burst are carrier extension. There is also additional overhead resulting from a mandatory interframe gap of 96 bits (non-data characters), plus the preamble, CRC and other non-data fields of each frame, but the total overhead can be kept to about 12% when frame bursting is used.

6.2.3 The 1000BASE-X Family of Ethernets

The 1000BASE-X Family includes those Gigabit Ethernets which use 8B/10B encoding. The 8 and the 10 of 8B/10B describe the width of the *data space* and *code space* respectively, and mean that a 8-bit data word is represented by a 10 bit code word.

The 1000BASE-X Family can be subdivided into three types:

1. **1000BASE-SX (shortwave):** The physical medium for this type of Ethernet is either 62.5 μm multimode or 50 μm multimode optical fiber. The wavelength of the laser drivers is 850 nm. The maximum distance supported is 260 m with 62.5 μm fiber and 525 m with 50 μm fiber.
2. **1000BASE-LX (longwave):** The physical medium for this type of Ethernet is 62.5 μm multimode, 50 μm multimode, or 10 mm single mode optical fiber. The wavelength of the laser drivers is 1300 nm. The maximum distance supported is 550 m with 62.5 mm or 50 μm fiber and 3000 km with 10 μm fiber.
3. **1000BASE-CX (copper):** The physical medium for this type of Ethernet is 150 Ω STP. The maximum distance supported is 25 m. The connector for all three types of fiber is the duplex SC. All three types of fiber are part of the EIA/TIA standard for building wiring. The connector for the type of cable used with a 1000BASE-CX device (called a copper jumper) is the high-speed serial data connector (HSSDC). Short copper jumpers are used for connecting 1000BASE-CX devices installed on racks, or placed in wiring closets.

The Ten Bit Interface

Clause 35 of the IEEE 802.3 standard defines the Gigabit medium independent interface (GMII) (see Fig. 6.9 on the next page). This is the 1000 mbps equivalent of the 10/100 mbps MII, however it was included more for the sake of consistency than as a practical interface. The GMII is seldom implemented, even as an interface between two ICs. The reason for this is that the 8B/10B encoder is more easily integrated with the MAC controller, which is digital, than with the transceiver, which is analog. The interface that is actually implemented is the one between the 8B/10B encoder/decoder and the transceiver, as shown in Fig. 6.9. This is referred to as the Ten Bit Interface.

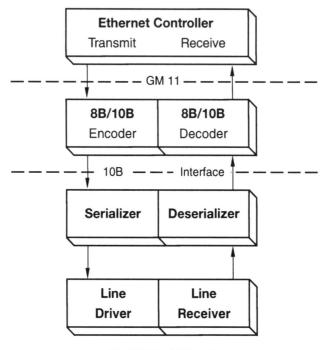

Fig. 6.9 Ten Bit Interface

The 1000BASE-T Ethernet, which is intended to work over 100 m twisted pairs, is still under development. But it is known that the 1000BASE-T will not use 8B/10B encoding. This means that 1000BASE-T devices will not work with the same interface, controller, and NIC as 1000BASE-X. However, the Ten Bit interface is still medium independent for any of the four types of media defined for the 1000BASE-X Family.

8B/10B Block Coding

The data bits of the 8B/10B code are denoted by A, B, C, D, E, F, G and H, while the code bits are denoted by a, b, c, d, e, f, g, h, i, and j.

The code space is divided into two groups:

1. The "K" group for the purpose of encoding control characters.
2. The "D" group for the purpose of encoding data bytes.

The special notation /Kx.y/ (control codes) and /Dx.y/ (data codes) is used, where x is the decimal value of EDCBA and y is the decimal value of HGF. Table 6.4 presents some examples of 8B/10B encoding.

Name	(8B Space) Byte Value	Data Word HGF EDCBA	Code Word abcdef fghi
/K28.5/	0xB3	101 11100	001111 1010
/D3.1/	0x23	001 00011	110001 1001
/D21.5/	0xB5	101 10101	101010 1010
/D23.2/	0x57	010 10111	111010 0101
			000101 0101
/D25.2/	0x59	010 11001	100110 0101
/D28.5/	0xB3	101 11100	001110 1010

Table 6.4 8B/10B Encoding Examples.

Running Disparity

The code words were selected (out of 1024 possible codes) to insure DC balance. For all code words, the number of 1s either equals the number of 0s, or the imbalance is at most one. Also, for every code word that has an imbalance, two code words were selected—one exactly balancing the other (see /D23.2/ in Table 6.4). The transmitter keeps a tally of the number of 1s and 0s, called the *running disparity*, and continuously selects the appropriate code word, preventing the imbalance from exceeding one.

Also the code words were selected so that the number of consecutive 1s or 0s never exceeds four. This was done to insure clock synchronization when used with NRZ line encoding.

Ordered Sets

1000BASE-X Ethernets use ordered sets to communicate control information. These ordered sets always begin with one of the code words that are members of the K group of control character (represented by the /Kx.y/ notation). For example, during an interframe gap, either the Idle 1 ordered set, or the Idle 2 ordered set, is transmitted (see Table 6.5). The Idle 1 ordered set is transmitted at first, if there is a running disparity that needs to be corrected. After that the Idle 2 ordered set is transmitted continuously.

Name	Description	Encoding	Length of Code Word in Bytes
/R/	Carrier Extend	/K23.7/	1
/S/	Start of Packet	/K27.7/	1
/T/	End of Packet	/K29.7/	1
/I1/	Idle 1	/K28.5/D5.6/	2
/I2/	Idle 2	/K28.5/D16.2/	2
/C1/	Configuration 1	/K28.5/D21.5/config-msg.	4
/C2/	Configuration 2	/K28.5/D2.2/config-msg.	4

Table 6.5 Ordered Sets

The /S/ ordered set, above, does not replace the preamble or starting frame delimeter, it simply indicates that the preamble of a new frame comes next.

1000BASE-X Auto-Negotiation

Auto-negotiation on 1000BASE-X devices does not concern itself with the special 6 mHz pulses used to negotiate signalling methods and data rates on 10/100 mbps Ethernets. This because there is no possibility of a RJ-45 connector being plugged into a 1000BASE-X device. Also, the 10 mbps devices that use SC connectors don't support auto-negotiation. It is simply assumed, when auto-negotiation begins, that the encoding method is 8B/10B, and that the correct connectors and transceivers have been configured manually.

An additional parameter is, however, introduced: flow control symmetry. The flow control negotiation is no longer limited to just flow control or no flow control—symmetric or asymmetric flow control can also be negotiated. Fig. 6.10 on the next page depicts the 16-bit page that is exchanged when 1000BASE-X devices are automatically con-figured to the highest common denominator.

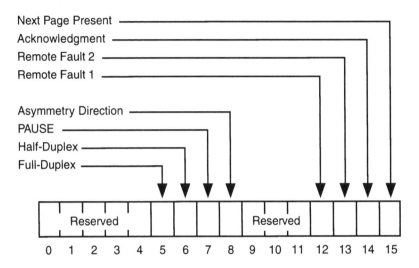

Fig. 6.10 Page Message Format for Auto-Negotiation of 1000 BASE-X

6.2.4 1000BASE-T Ethernets

Gigabit Ethernets that will rely upon Category 5 UTP as the trans-mission medium are now under development. The data and line encod-ing schemes have not yet been defined, but it is known that the maxi-mum distance will be 100 m (maximum extent 200 m).

Since 10/100 mbps Ethernet devices will be pluggable into 1000BASE-T devices—all three will be using RJ-45 connectors—it is important that 1000BASE-T auto-negotiation be backward compatible. The protocol used for auto-negotiation on 10/100 mbps Ethernets will be extended to allow 1000BASE-T devices to negotiate data rates, sig-nalling methods, flow control, etc.

6.3 Integrated Services Digital Network (ISDN)

The transmission of voice over public telephone networks has been completely digitized except for the local loop which connects business or residence telephones with central office switches. The next logical step in the evolution of telecommunications is the universal installation of a digital connection from the central office to the subscriber. The idea of ISDN is to complete this evolutionary process from analog to digital, and at the same time fully integrate the telephone network so that a full spectrum of digital services such as voice, data (circuit-switched or packet-switched), fax, and even video are available over a single standard telephone outlet.

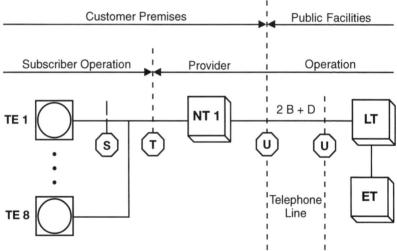

Fig. 6.11 ISDN Basic Access Connection

Fig. 6.11 depicts the basic structure of an ISDN connection.

At both the subscriber end and the central office there are conversion functions. On the subscriber's premises, line terminal equipment referred to as *network termination 1* (NT1) provides the interface between terminal equipment (TE) and the transmission line. At the central office, line termination equipment (LT) connects the exchange termination (ET) with the subscriber line.

Part of the motivation for ISDN is to take full advantage of the millions of twisted pairs that are already in place. This is accomplished by what is called a U chip, which is used in both NT1 equipment and LT equipment (see reference points U, Fig. 6.11). The U chip at one end transmits a dummy frame on one line of a twisted pair while the U chip at the other end transmits real data on the twisted pair's other line. Because the dummy frame is known to the transmitting U chip, it is able to exactly compensate, substantially increasing the capacity of the twisted pair. The disadvantage to this technique is that both of the twisted pair cables are needed for one-way transmission, thus full-duplex transmission requires two twisted pairs.

At reference point T, shown in Fig. 6.11, the characteristics of the interface are:

1. a four-wire interface consisting of one transmitting pair and one receiving pair.
2. a user transmission rate of 144 kbps that includes three channels, two B channels of 64 kbps and one D channel of 16 kbps. Channel D is used to support the signalling system: "Digital Signalling System 1" (DSS-1).
3. a total transmission rate of 192 kbps, with the difference being 48 kbps used to control the passive medium to which the TE equipment is connected (activation of terminals, bus contention resolution, etc.).

The TE equipment may include digital telephones, facsimile machines capable of fast fax service, PCs, terminals, and even slow scan video.

There are two advantages to using channel D for signalling: (1) a digital signalling service is faster allowing end-to-end connections to be made in 100 ms or less, and (2) the decoupling of the signalling system from the data transport allows signalling during a call. ISDN calls may be multimedia—for example, a call may include a fax, or an exchange of computer data, with one B channel used for the voice call, the other for the fax or the computer data, and the DSS-1 signalling system used to make the connection across the telephone network and also to control access to the TE equipment.

DSS-1 is separated into two levels. The network level permits establishment and clearing of connections similar to the way the X.25 network level establishes virtual circuits. The connections established for the two B channels are, however, circuit-switched. The network level messages are carried in link level, LAP-D, frames, which are similar to the X.25 LAP-D. The LAP-D frame is shown in Fig. 6.12.

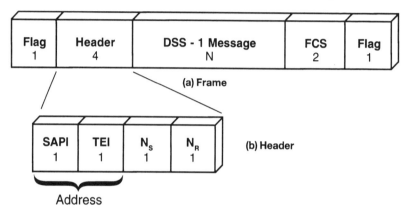

Fig. 6.12 LAP–D Frame

The two address fields of an LAP-D frame are the service access point identifier (SAPI), which identifies the type of message, and the terminal equipment identifier (TEI), as shown in Fig. 6.12(b). If the SAPI = 0, it is a message to establish or clear an associated B channel connection, and the address of the subscriber interface will be contained in the DSS-1 message (see Fig. 6.12 (a)). The address of subscriber interfaces is contained in the DSS-1 message. The subscriber addresses are E.164 numbers issued by the ITU-T, and include fields for country and region. The TEI addresses in the LAP-D frame will activate a particular device—for example, a fax machine can be activated without the telephone ringing.

Although the B channels are circuit switched, whether they are used for isochronous digital data such as voice, or for non-isochronous data such as a file transfer, or a terminal transaction, the D channel can, in addition to signalling, be used for packet-switched transmission of user data.

6.3.1 Primary Rate Interface (PRI)

Primary rate interface consists of twenty-three 64 Kbps B channels and one 64 Kbps D channel (used for signalling), for a total of 1.536 mbps—the equivalent of a T1 line. PRI access can support, when NT2 line terminal equipment is used, up to 50 TE devices, including a private branch exchange (PBX).

6.3.2 Broadband ISDN

Broadband ISDN, still in the developmental stage, supports transmission rates of the SONET hierarchy (see Table 6.1 on page 149). While basic ISDN has been a little slow to catch on, a completely integrated digital telephone network supporting voice, fax, data, and video will eventually become a reality.

Broadband ISDN, which will operate at transmission rates of 100 mbps and beyond, will someday be almost universally available, offering services such as full motion video telephony.

6.4 Asynchronous Transfer Mode (ATM)

ISDN as it is currently being implemented is not truly an integrated network. Although there may be one port for the transmission of voice and circuit-switched digital data on the B channels and packet-switched digital data the D channel, ISDN is really being implemented by multiple networks, as shown in Fig. 6.13.

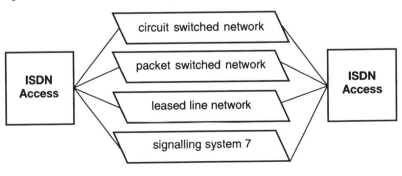

Fig. 6.13 ISDN Subnetworks

If one considers that in addition to multiple ISDN networks there are also SMDS networks, public X.25 networks, private X.25 networks, frame relay, etc., it becomes pretty clear that telecommunications is nowhere near the ITU-T Study Group 13's goal of a completely integrated network for voice, fax, digital data, and video.

6.4.1   The ATM Concept

Early experiments with transmitting voice over packet-switching networks were unsuccessful, due to the unusually high sensitivity of speech data to delays. Video is another type of data that is sensitive to delays. Both voice and video are, however, relatively tolerant of errors. If one bit out of ten thousand is corrupted, the transmitted voice or video is not noticeably affected.

On the other hand, data is more tolerant of delays. An occasional half second delay, which would garble speech, makes no difference for data. But data is, however, intolerant of errors. For most forms of data, any corrupted bits at all are unacceptable.

The idea of ATM is to integrate the transmission of delay-sensitive and error-sensitive data into a single fast packet-switching network that takes advantage of the high reliability of fiber optic transmission. The basic unit of data transport over this network is the 53 byte *ATM cell,* shown in Fig. 6.14.

Header 5 bytes

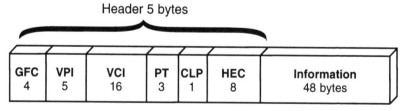

GFC	VPI	VCI	PT	CLP	HEC	Information
4	5	16	3	1	8	48 bytes

Note: Values in header fields represent number of bits

Fig. 6.14 ATM Cell

The fields of the ATM cell have the following significance:

1.   **Generic Flow Control (GFC)** - use of this field is still under study.

2. **Virtual Path Identifier (VPI)** - identifies a *virtual path* between sites or within an ATM network.
3. **Virtual Channel Identifier (VCI)** - identifies a *virtual channel* between end-points.
4. **Payload Type (PT)** - The main purpose of the PT field is to distinguish between cells containing user data and network information.
5. **Cell Loss Priority (CLP)** - The CLP field allows a two-level loss priority, 0 and 1. Cells with priority 1 should be discarded before cells with priority 0, should congestion occur.
6. **Header Error Control (HEC)** - The HEC field provides a CRC check for error protection of the header. It is capable of detecting all header errors and correcting all single bit errors. There is no error protection of the payload (data) field.
7. **Payload** - This field contains the data to be transmitted.

The reason the ITU-T's Study Group decided on a small, uniform, 53-byte cell is to make it statistically much less likely that a cell containing voice or video data will be unacceptably delayed at switching nodes. If variable-length frames were allowed, a large frame could slip in ahead of a delay sensitive cell—at a switching node—resulting in a much longer delay. With 53-byte ATM cells, as long as congestion is not present, every cell is output almost immediately at a switching node.

Intermediate nodes in an ATM network are switches rather than routers. Virtual circuits are established across the network prior to transmission of end-to-end data. This allows the VPI and VCI fields of an ATM cell to be much smaller because they don't have to identify a unique destination on a network, only the next link on a virtual path or virtual channel. This contributes to the overall compactness of the ATM cell. Also, because a virtual circuit has been established, the routing decision has already been made, requiring only a quick table lookup.

ATM takes advantage of reliable, modern transmission by performing minimal error checking at switching nodes. The HEC field shown in Fig. 6.14 is for checking of the header only. If an uncorrectable header error is detected, the cell is discarded. This allows a header field of only eight bytes. The minimal amount of error checking allows very fast switching at network nodes. There is no checking for sequence errors. This is done at the end-points of the network, usually by the user. However, because the virtual circuit model is used, the cells that do arrive are in sequence.

In order to understand the ATM concept, it is important to grasp the meaning of the term *asynchronous transfer mode.* ATM has multiplexing capability. It multiplexes and mixes cells from multiple users on a single transmission link. Fig. 6.15 shows a comparison of time division multiplexing (TDM), which is synchronous, and ATM multiplexing, which is asynchronous. TDM keeps track of data by time slots, thus wasting bandwidth that could be used for data that is ready to be transmitted. ATM transmits a cell when it is ready, or *asynchronously.*

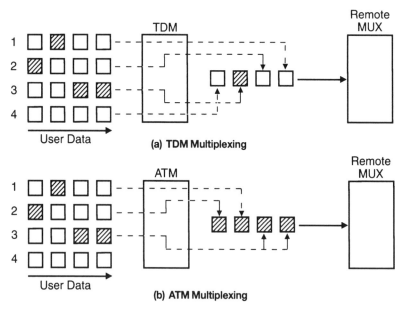

Fig. 6.15 TDM vs. ATM Multiplexing

As far as where the phrase *transfer mode* came from, an example of earlier transfer mode was the telegraph network. The infrastructure of the telegraph network included non-insulated iron wires. If two stations were not directly connected, a message was relayed from one station to another, until it reached its destination. When the telephone network replaced the telegraph network as the primary mode of communication, it was necessary to install insulated copper wire to provide the quality of transmission required for voice. Long distance calls could not be relayed, so direct connections were required—that took three or four minutes for operators to set up, using manual switches. The point is that these were two different transfer modes, thus the telephone system required a new infrastructure and method of operation.

ATM, to work the way it is intended, will require very fast, high-quality transmission, probably over optical fiber, and switching systems that are designed to make almost instantaneous routing decisions.

6.4.2 Virtual Path Identifiers/Virtual Channel Identifiers (VPIs/VCIs)

The VPI and VCI fields have the same purpose as the logical channel numbers (LCN) of X.25 except that ATM has two virtual circuit identifiers to provide greater flexibility. The VCI identifies a virtual channel between end-systems. Virtual paths are not end-to-end. VPIs are used to multiplex together a number of virtual channels that share a virtual path for part of the end-to-end connection.

VPIs/VCIs are similar to the virtual circuit numbers (VCNs) described in Section 4.1.2 on page 101. Switching nodes will often, as was shown in Fig. 4.2 on page 104, use a different VCN for the next hop, if the outgoing VCN was already taken by another virtual circuit. Along a virtual path the VPIs have significance and often change from hop to hop, with the VCNs just along for the ride. When the end of the virtual path has been reached, the VCNs have significance, and they change from hop to hop.

Fig. 6.16(a) on the next page shows one the most common uses of these connection identifiers, especially if ATM is used to connect remote LANs. As shown in Fig. 6.16(a), the VPIs have significance along a virtual path, and thus have a tendency to change from hop to hop. This example allows subscribers use of the unchanged VCNs so they can implement their own virtual channels. This configuration only allows up to 256 links between a site and the first network node, because the VPI field is only one byte. After the first node on the network, the GFC field is not used, allowing a 16-bit VPI, thus the VPI field can identify up to 4096 links between network nodes.

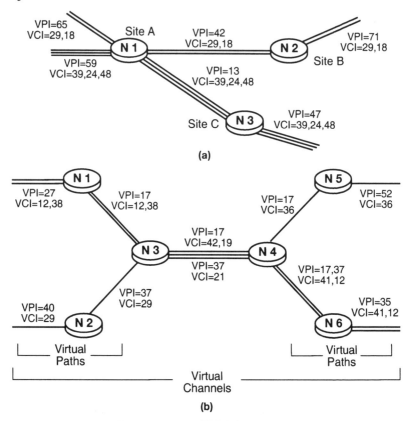

Fig. 6.16 Use of VPI, VCI Identifiers

Another possibility is to allow the ATM network use of both VPI and VCI identifiers in order to set up a virtual connection between two end-systems. If both identifiers are used, there is a virtual channel from between end-systems, with virtual paths within the virtual channel. With this configuration, the VCIs would have significance and could change between virtual paths and the VPIs would have significance and could often change from hop to hop along the virtual path, as shown in Fig. 6.16(b).

The examples shown in Fig. 6.16 could be agreed upon by the user and the ATM network at subscription time—the ATM equivalent of a permanent virtual circuits (PVC)—or they could be set up at the time of the call by ATM signalling. They could also be a hybrid, with the VPIs in Fig. 6.16(a) permanent, and the VCIs used to set up a virtual channel at the time of the call.

6.4.3 Broadband ISDN Architecture

The architecture of B-ISDN consists of three "planes": (1) the user plane, (2) the control plane, and (3) the management plane, as shown in Fig. 6.17.

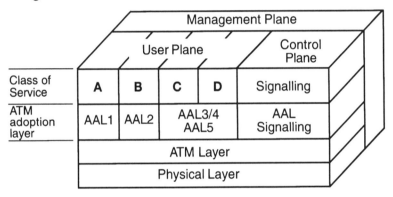

Fig. 6.17 B–ISDN Architecture

Management Plane

The management plane is transparent to user nodes and performs such functions as:

1. the dynamic detection, isolation, and correction of node and link failures.
2. performance management - monitoring and reporting system performance.
3. the reporting of information on network usage for billing.

Management cells, which are transmitted between ATM switches only, are identified by the PT field. For example, PT = 4 indicates segment operations and management (OAM) and PT = 5 indicates end-to-end OAM.

Control Plane

The most important function of the control plane is the signalling of a network's nodes to establish, maintain, and release virtual path connections/virtual channel connections (VPCs/VCCs). There are four dedicated signalling virtual channels (SVCs) that are used to send signalling messages between the user and the *user node interface* (UNI).

Preassigned VCIs are used to identify SVC cells. Cells with VCI = 5 and VPI = 0 are used to negotiate end-point to end-point VPCs/VCCs. When a virtual circuit is established between end-points it must be negotiated not only with the UNI, but also with each of *network node interfaces* (NNIs) making up the virtual circuit. If the negotiation is successful, a bidirectional switched virtual connection is established, with the VPIs/VCIs that support that connection entered into the network node's routing tables (see Fig. 6.16(b)).

A metasignalling virtual channel is also available, identified by VCI = 1. This SVC is used for point-to-multi-point connections—a possible application could be teleconferencing. This SVC also can be used to modify the point-to-multi-point virtual connection, i.e., add or disconnect endpoints.

In addition to these two bidirectional SVCs, there are also two unidirectional SVCs from the ATM network to the users. One is a broadcast SVC and the other is a group SVC. Both are used to signal users in the same service class profile.

User Plane

The user plane consists of the hierarchical structure of the physical layer, the ATM layer, the ATM adaption layer (AAL), and the higher layers.

ATM Adaption Layer (AAL)

The ATM adaption layer (AAL) has two sublayers: (1) the convergence sublayer (CS), and (2) the segmentation and reassembly sublayer (SAR).

The convergence sublayer provides the mechanism for mixing input data with different requirements such as voice, video, and data. The convergence sublayer defines four classes of service:

1. Class A - a constant bit rate (CBR) service for the transmission of voice or video.
2. Class B - a variable bit rate (VBR) service for delay sensitive data such as compressed audio or video.
3. Class C - a connection-oriented service data with variable delays.
4. Class D - a connectionless service with variable delays.

The format of the data received by the CS may be a bit stream, as in the case of class A, or it may be PDUs from other data services such as TCP/IP, SMDS, and frame relay. The PDUs may be in the form of frames, packets, or datagrams. It is the job of the CS to map the diverse data it receives onto five AALs: AAL1, AAL2, AAL 3/4, and AAL5.

The CS accepts data of various types, forms the appropriate CS PDU for that service class, and hands it to the SAR sublayer. The SAR segments the CS PDU into what will be the payload field of ATM cells, and passes the SAR PDU to the ATM layer, which adds the header. The control information added to the CS PDU and SAR PDU allows the AAL to provide the *quality of service* (QOS) required for a specific service.

Fig. 6.18 on the next page shows the operation of the AAL1, which could be used for CBR data such as voice.

The SAR PDU fields in Fig. 6.18 have the following significance:

1. **Sequence Number (SN)** - This field includes a 3-bit sequence number and a convergence sublayer indication (CSI) bit, which indicates the presence of a convergence sublayer.
2. **Sequence Number Protection (SNP)** - The SNP consists of a 3-bit CRC and one parity bit, for protection of the SN.

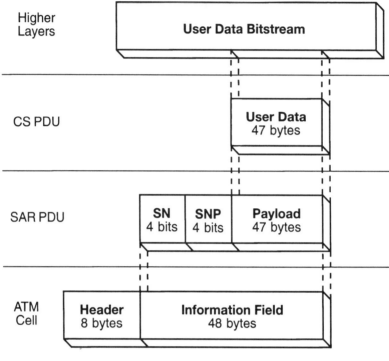

Fig. 6.18 AALI Operation

Fig. 6.19 on the next page shows the operation of the AAL3/4, which could be used for a connectionless, delay-tolerant data service.

The significance of the CS PDU fields in Fig. 6.19 are the following:

1. **Common Part Indicator (CPI)** - indicates the measurements for the BAsize field.
2. **Beginning Tag (Btag)** - indicates misassemble if different from the Etag field.
3. **Buffer Allocation Size (BA Size)** - the size of the buffer needed to receive the CS PDU, usually the same as the length of the Data Field.
4. **Padding (PAD)** - the PAD field insures the CS PDU is an exact multiple of four bytes.

5. **Alignment (AL)** - a byte of zeros to make the trailer aligned with four bytes.
6. **Ending Tag (Etag)** - this should be same as the Btag field.
7. **Length (LN)** - length of data field in bytes.

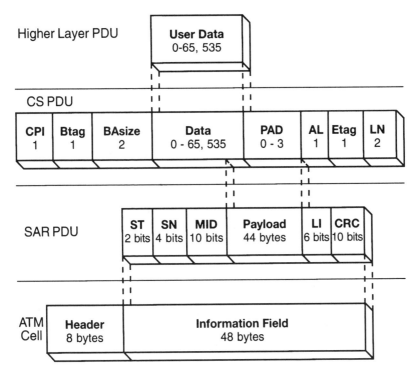

Fig. 6.19 AAL3/4 Operation

The significance of the SAR PDU fields in Fig. 6.19 is the following:

1. **Sequence Number (SN)** - used for sequencing.
2. **Multiplexing Identification (MID)** - identifies the CS PDU when different CS PDUs are multiplexed.
3. **Length Indication (LI)** - length of user data in payload.
4. **CRC** - CRC calculated over entire SAR PDU.

ATM Layer

The operations performed by the ATM layer of the control plane include:

1. the multiplexing and mixing of cells over the same physical link.
2. the translation of incoming VPI and VCI identifiers to the proper pair for the output link.
3. the generation and interpretation of cell headers at network end-systems.

Physical Layer (PHY)

The physical layer (PHY) is responsible for the transmission of cells over a physical medium. ATM was initially aimed at SONET STS-1 (51.84 mbps) and STS-3 (155 mbps). However, ATM over shielded and unshielded twisted pairs are also being implemented. The PHY must provide the appropriate bit encoding—for example, Manchester code— for the physical link. If SONET is used, the PHY must pack the cells into outgoing SONET frames, and unpack them for processing at the next node.

6.4.4 Quality of Service (QOS)

The agreed quality of service (QOS) is negotiated by the end-system and the ATM network at the time of a signalling connection, or, in the case of a PVC, by network management and the user at subscription time.

QOS parameters include:

1. peak rate in bits per second.
2. maximum time of peak rate in bits per second.
3. average throughput in bits per second.
4. maximum acceptable delay in seconds, or fractions of a second.

A data application may require both a high peak rate and a high throughput, but the requirements for maximum acceptable delay may be flexible. A CBR voice application's peak rate may be the same as the average throughput, but its requirements for maximum acceptable delay would be stringent. A VBR application for compressed video may require a much higher peak rate than average throughput, with a low acceptable delay.

In order to guarantee the agreed upon QOS for each virtual connection, ATM relies on preventive rather than reactive measures. Although control plane cells may include a *forward explicit congestion notification* (FECN), this is considered too slow for most applications. To avoid congestion, cells are discarded at network nodes, with the cells with CLP = 1 discarded first. This allows, for example, voice applications to set the CLP bit to 1 for those cells which affect the quality of speech the least, allowing a worst case scenario of graceful degradation.

Other preventive QOS measures include:

1. **Connection Admission Control** - If the QOS cannot be guaranteed, because of high network congestion, the connection is not accepted.
2. **User Parameter Control** - Users are policed to ensure they do not exceed QOS parameters. If a user is exceeding agreed parameters, the user's cells may have the CLP set to 1 so they will be among the first to be discarded, if a node becomes overwhelmed. In an extreme case, the user may be disconnected.
3. **Cell Loss Priority** - The negotiation between the user and the network may result in the user agreeing to set the CLP bit to 1 for a certain percentage of cells.

Problem Solving Example:

 What is meant by the phrase "statistical sharing of resources" associated with ATM?

If a network has many traffic streams, the probability of a theoretical peak rate—all traffic streams at their peak rate simultaneously—is very low. When the rare occurrence of a peak rate occurs, ATM momentarily discards non-delay-sensitive cells until the network settles back to a normal level. This greatly increases efficiency, because the network does not have to be designed for a worst case scenario that almost never happens.

6.4.5 Data Exchange Interface (DXI)

The *data exchange interface* (DXI) performs a function similar to a PAD on an X.25 network. It is a kind of DSU/CSU that allows several computers to be connected and communicate with computers on the other side of an ATM network.

A DXI utilizes hardware to manufacture cells very rapidly. The idea of the DXI is to lower cost by not requiring each computer to have its own cell manufacturing capability.

6.5 Frame Relay

ITU-T recommendation X.25 has proven to be a successful vehicle for packet-switching networks. Access speeds to X.25 networks can be increased from DS-0 (64 kbps), which is most common. However, the architecture of X.25 is not well-suited for high-speed switching with minimum delay.

The X.25 standard was developed at a time when public transmission facilities were much less resistant to noise and other factors which can cause corruption of data. The design of the X.25 architecture resulted in protocols that require considerable processing to guard against transmission errors. Even after an LAP-D frame has been checked at the data-link level, the encapsulated packet is checked for sequence errors at the network level. X.25 requires about thirty processing steps. Also, an X.25 frame cannot be forwarded until it has been processed.

Fast-packet switching is a technique that forwards a packet while it is still being received. *Frame relay* is one technique that allows fast-packet switching, others being SMDS and ATM (SMDS and ATM are closely related). The difference between frame relay and the SMDS/ATM philosophy is that the former transmits fixed size 53 octet cells, while frame relay transmits variable sized, longer LAP-D frames.

Actually, the protocols for frame relay were being developed when it was part of the ISDN implementation, and as a result the LAP-D link layer protocol was used.

In addition to having the advantage of fast-packet switching, frame relay only requires a half-dozen steps to check a frame for errors. If an error is found and the frame is already being forwarded, the intermediate node aborts it immediately and sends an abort message downstream. This should result in the frame eventually disappearing from the network. However, if the frame eventually arrives at its destination, the host will request a retransmission anyway.

Frame relay relies upon end-to-end sequence and error control, which is only infrequently required because today's transmission facilities, particularly those with optical fiber supports, are much less susceptible to interference.

Fig. 6.20 shows a core LAP-D frame and the address fields.

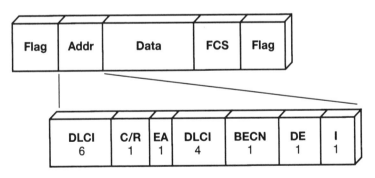

Fig. 6.20 Core LAP-D Frame

The fields of the address field of a core LAP-D frame have the following significance:

1. **DLCI: Data Link Connection Identifier** - a total of ten bits in the first and fourth fields (see Fig. 6.20). This is used to identify a permanent virtual circuit.

2. **C/R: Command/Response** - not used in frame relay.
3. **EA: Extended Address** - this indicates the address field is continued in the next octet.
4. **FECN: Forward Explicit Congestion Notification** - indicates if frames traveling in the same direction may be affected by congestion.
5. **BECN: Backward Explicit Congestion Notification** - signifies possible congestion for frames traveling in the opposite direction.
6. **DE: Discard Eligibility** - indicates if a frame should be discarded in preference to other frames if congestion is present.

CHAPTER 7

The Internet

An internet is a virtual network built by interconnecting a number of individual physical networks that might employ different data-link technologies. These networks may be remote LANs connected through X.25, ATM, or frame relay networks, or by a dedicated link, such as a T1 line. This network may be connected to a *regional network,* which may be in turn be attached to a *national backbone network.* Finally, this national backbone may be connected to other national backbone networks, forming an international network.

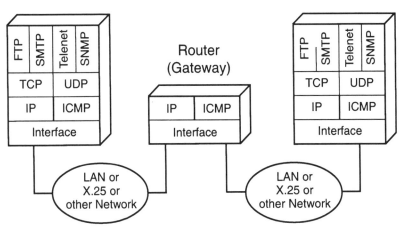

Fig. 7.1 Internet Protocol Suite (Route across two networks)

The Internet is the premier global network that uses the TCP/IP suite of protocols that was pioneered in the 1970s by the Defense Department's Advanced Research Project Agency Network (ARPANET). Fig. 7.1 on the previous page depicts the basic structure of an internet and the TCP/IP protocol suite.

There is a distinction between a router and a gateway (see Fig. 7.1). A router consists of the hardware and software needed to connect two subnetworks at the network level. A gateway provides protocol conversion from one technologically different network to another. Gateways may operate at the transport layer level or above.

The interface layer shown in Fig. 7.1 corresponds to the data-link and physical layers of the OSI Model. The interface layer performs functions such as the mapping of network addresses to data-link addresses.

The Internet protocol (IP) is equivalent to the network layer of the OSI Model. The IP layer will accept a datagram from the TCP layer and route it across a concatenation of physical networks to a remote TCP layer. The *Internet control message protocol* (ICMP) provides basic management functions at the network level.

The transmission control protocol (TCP) provides for the establishment of a reliable connection between user applications on host computers. The TCP functions are equivalent to the transport layer of the OSI Model. The "user datagram protocol" (UDP) provides a connectionless transport layer service as an alternative to TCP.

7.1   Definition of the Internet

There is some confusion about what the Internet is. If an interconnected network operates with the TCP/IP protocol suite, it is an internet. If one of its hosts has an IP address that was assigned at the Internet Assigned Numbers Authority (IANA) and it is reachable at that address by Internet routers, than that host is on the Internet. In other words there is an overlap between various internets and the Internet.

7.2 A Brief History of the Internet

In 1983 the ARPANET was split in two, with the MILNET to be used for military purposes and the ARPANET to continue computer network research.

The development of the Internet was furthered by the National Science Foundation Network (NSFNET). The NSFNET was created to connect six supercomputer sites using the TCP/IP protocol. The NSF furthered its efforts into the creation of a backbone network and provided funding for the development of regional networks.

By 1986 the NSFNET consisted of a 56 kbps backbone connecting six supercomputers with eight regional networks. This allowed university computer science departments around the country to access supercomputers. In 1987, the NSFNET awarded the contract to operate the backbone network to the Michigan Education and Research Triad (Merit, Inc). Merit operated the backbone in conjunction with IBM and MCI. The backbone trunks were upgraded to T1 lines (1.54 mbps) in 1989 and further to fiber optic T3 lines (44.736 mbps) in 1992.

In 1990 the NSFNET assumed much of the functionality of the original ARPANET, which ceased to exist.

Fig. 7.2 (on next page) shows the topology of a mid-level regional network which is connected to the Internet.

Actually Fig. 7.2 may be a bit misleading in that a mid-level regional network may comprise as many as two or three hundred companies, universities, and governmental agencies in a three or four state region. However, the basic concept is this: all the organizations that make up the regional network are interconnected to each other through lower capacity leased lines (19.2 kbps, 56 kbps, 1.54 mbps), with a higher capacity fiber optic T3 line (44.736 mbps) carrying traffic to and from the regional network to a national backbone network, which is in turn connected to the worldwide Internet.

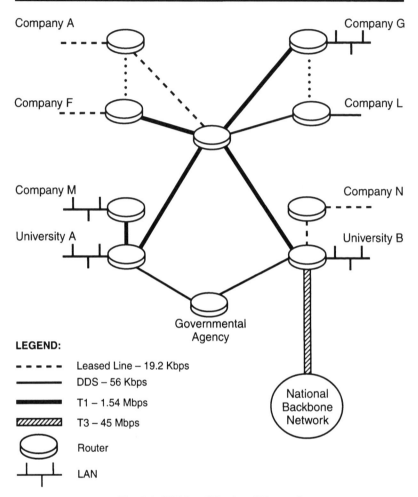

Fig. 7.2 Mid-level Regional Network

Some national backbone trunks have been upgraded to STS-3 (155.52 mbps) and there are plans to eventually migrate to STS-12 (622.08 mbps).

7.3   The Transport Layer

The transport layer of the Internet suite provides basically the same services as the transport layer of the OSI model with a few important exceptions:

1. **Connectionless Option** - While the OSI transport layer is connection oriented, TCP/IP offers the option of a connectionless, datagram service at this level—UDP.
2. **Stream-oriented** - The data transfer offered to higher layers by the OSI Model is packet-oriented (SDUs), while the most commonly used transport protocol of the Internet suite, TCP, offers a stream-oriented (series of octets) virtual "pipeline" service.
3. **Graceful Release** - TCP has the capability of a "graceful release," while OSI leaves this to the higher layers.

The main idea of the transport layer, for both OSI and the Internet suite, is to provide a reliable end-to-end data transport service for the higher layers. OSI does this for the higher layers, while TCP/IP provides this service for the application layer, with a connectionless option—UDP.

7.3.1 Transport Control Protocol (TCP)

Of the two Internet transport layer protocols, TCP and UDP, TCP is the protocol that is most often used, and the one that provides a reliable end-to-end service for the application layer. The service provided by TCP is characterized by:

1. **Full Duplex** - TCP allows application entities the transfer of a sequence of octets—a "stream"—in both directions simultaneously.
2. **Connection Establishment** - TCP establishes a virtual connection between two application entities resident on two host computers. A connection has three phases: the establishment phase, the data transfer phase, and the release phase.
3. **Error Free Data** - TCP guarantees that user data is delivered in sequence and free of corruption.

The TCP Connection Establishment Phase
When TCP establishes a connection there must be a unique way to identify that connection. TCP messages are called *segments.* In order to insure that each segment that is sent or received is related to the

connection to which it belongs, connections are identified by the following:

1. **Source port number** - The application entity on the source host computer, for which TCP is establishing the connection, is identified by a 16-bit binary number called the source port number.
2. **Destination port number** - The application entity on the destination host, that is the target of the connection, is identified by the destination port number.
3. **Source network address** - The source host computer is identified on the Internet by a 32-bit network address.
4. **Destination network address** - The destination host computer is identified by a thirty-two bit network address. When TCP sends a segment, it hands the network address to the network layer—to the Internet Protocol (IP). For this reason the network address is usually referred to as the IP address.

The combination of a port number and an IP address is called a socket. The source socket includes the source port number and the source IP address. The destination socket includes the destination port number and the destination IP address. A connection is uniquely identified by a 96-bit quantity that includes the source socket and the destination socket.

Sockets make possible multiplexing of transport connections, which is made necessary by several users attempting to communicate simultaneously with the host, or several host processes attempting to communicate. Multiple entities within the TCP layer support multiplexing.

When an Internet connection is established the following events occur:

1. The TCP entity is initially in a "closed" state. When it receives an indication from an application entity that it is willing to accept a connection for a specific port number, the TCP entity changes state to "listen"—this is called a "passive open" state.

2. The application entity requests a connection with a remote application entity which it identifies by a socket number. The TCP entity changes state to "active open" and stores the socket number in the TCP control block.
3. The TCP selects a sequence number. Sequence numbers are used to keep track of the octets that make up the data stream during the data transfer phase. The TCP also stores the sequence number in the TCP *control block.*
4. The TCP forms a SYN segment which includes the source and destination port numbers and the sequence number. The SYN segment, along with the destination IP address, is handed to the IP, which routes it to the destination host.
5. The remote TCP determines if the application entity identified by that port number will accept the connection. If it will, it selects its own sequence number and sends back a SYN/ACK segment.
6. Upon receiving the SYN/ACK segment, the initiating TCP sends an ACK segment. This completes a "three-way handshake," and the connection is established.

At this point, both the initiating and accepting TCP entities have each other's sequence numbers (which are 16 bits), and their own, stored in their respective TCP control blocks. The sequence number can be used to keep track of the data stream and can also be used for acknowledgments.

The TCP Data Transfer Phase
The TCP provides for the application layer a full-duplex virtual circuit data transfer service with the stream of octets delivered in sequence and free of errors.

In order to maximize throughput, a "pipelining" effect is achieved by both communicating TCPs informing the other, by means of a window number, how many octets they can accept without an acknowledgment.

The format of a TCP segment is shown in Fig. 7.3(a) on the next page.

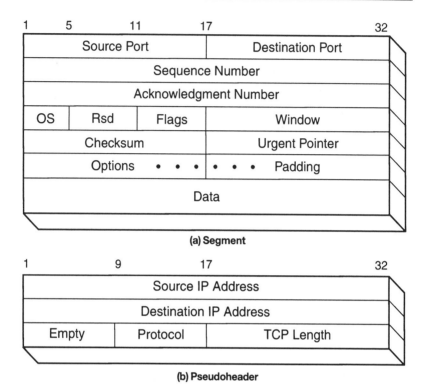

Fig. 7.3 TCP Segment

The significance of the fields of a TCP segment are:

1. **Source Port** - identification of the source port.
2. **Destination Port** - identification of the destination port.
3. **Sequence Number** - sequence number of the first octet in this segment, unless the SYN bit is set in the flag field. If the SYN bit is set, it is the initial sequence number.
4. **Acknowledgment Number** - the sequence number of the next octet the TCP expects to be acknowledged, if the ACK bit of the flag field is set.
5. **DO: Data Offset** - the length of header in 32-bit words.
6. **RSD:** Reserved for future use.
7. **Flags** - There are six bits in the flag field which have the following significance:

- **URG** - signifies urgent data, similar to OSI expedited data.
- **ACK** - signifies acknowledgment (see 4).
- **PHS** - request by remote TCP for local TCP to "push" all data it has been buffering to the application entity.
- **RST** - Reset the connection.
- **SYN** - signifies SYN segment (see 3).
- **FIN** - No more data will be sent.

8. **Window** - the number of octets beginning with the one specified in the acknowledgment field that the sender is willing to accept.

9. **Checksum** - the 1s complement modulus ($2**16 - 1$) of all the sixteen bit words in the segment plus the *pseudoheader* shown in Fig. 7.3(b)—the pseudoheader is not part of the segment, but is implicit in the information handed to the internet layer.

10. **Urgent Pointer** - pointer to the last octet of the urgent data.

11. **Options** - This field contains zero or more options.

12. **Padding** - pads the header to an even number of thirty-two bit words.

13. **Data** - contains zero or more octets of data—not necessarily a multiple of four octets.

Although the TCP provides a virtual circuit service for the application layer, the service provided for the TCP by the network layer, the IP, is of the connectionless datagram type. With some IP datagrams being lost or discarded, the TCP must emulate reliability by setting a timer after each segment, then retransmitting if and when the timer expires.

The TCP Release Phase

After the application entity indicates to the TCP that it has sent all of its data, the TCP finishes sending all outstanding data, setting the FIN bit in the flag field of the last segment. When the remote TCP receives the FIN segment, it informs its application entity and acknowledges the FIN. After all outstanding data segments have been acknowledged, including the FINs, the connection is released. This is a graceful release.

A TCP may perform an ungraceful release by sending a RST segment, then immediately aborting.

7.3.2 The UDP Protocol

The user datagram protocol provides a connectionless datagram service at the transport level. As the UDP does little more than utilize the services of the IP, a UDP packet does not have nearly as many fields as a TCP segment, as shown in Fig. 7.4.

| 1 | 17 | 32 |

Source Port	Destination Port
Length	Checksum
Data	

Fig. 7.4 UDP Datagram

The fields of the UDP packet depicted in Fig. 7.4 are self-explanatory and have the same significance as the corresponding fields in the TCP segment, with the exception of the length field, which refers to the length of the packet header plus the data field in octets. The checksum is a ones complement checksum computed over the entire UDP packet plus the pseudoheader—the pseudoheader is the same as the one used for the TCP checksum.

7.4 The Internet Layer

The internet layer is inherently "stateless." There is no attempt to keep track of datagrams as they are propagated across a network. Communication, between intermediate nodes, or routers as they are called, is connectionless.

As a result, datagrams can be lost, reordered, or duplicated. If a datagram is found to be corrupted, it is discarded. Likewise, datagrams are discarded if they exceed their "lifetime" or if a node is congested. Part of the design philosophy of the Internet suite is to place minimal demands on the internet layer. For this reason, there must be protocols at higher layers that are responsible for maintaining a reliable connection, on an end-to-end basis.

If the TCP is used, the transport layer is responsible for the reliability of the end-to-end connection. This responsibility could also be the application layer's, if the UDP is chosen as the transport protocol. The philosophy of the Internet suite is that it is more efficient to concentrate reliability functions in one layer, thus avoiding redundancy. The TCP performs whatever resequencing and recovery is required when datagrams arrive out of order, or are lost.

However, Internet protocols rely primarily on the interface layer, which is described in the next section, for data integrity. At the interface layer there are usually powerful CRC algorithms implemented in hardware. The checksums performed by the transport and the internet layers are to guard against software bugs or serious hardware malfunctions, rather than to detect all single bit errors caused by such factors as noise.

7.4.1 Internet Addressing

There are two kinds of devices attached to an internet: hosts and routers. A host is not responsible for forwarding or routing, and will generally only have one attachment to the network. A router will have more than one attachment, and may be attached to more than one network. For every attachment there is an internet address. A device with more than one address is said to be *multi-homed.*

An Internet address has 32-bits and is broken down into five categories, with the three most important shown in Table 7.1. An Internet address is usually referred to as an IP address because it is used by the IP protocol.

Class	Number of Bits	
	Network	Host
A	7	24
B	14	16
C	21	8

Table 7.1 Internet Address Classes

For class A, there are 128 potential networks, each with 16 million hosts. For class B, there are 16,384 potential networks, each with around 64,000 hosts. For class C, there are two million potential networks, each with 254 hosts. For class A and class B, it is difficult to get a petition approved by the Internet Assigned Numbers Authority (IANA). It is worth noting that this address structure allows for three and a half billion potential devices, and even allowing for many of the addresses being assigned to multi-homed routers rather than hosts, there is still room for a great deal of growth.

Two Level Address

Network Identifier	Host Identifier

Network Identifier	Subnet	Host

Subnet Address

(a)

Network Identifier	Subnet	Host

1 1 1 1 1 1 1 1 1 1 1 1 1 1 1 1 1 1 1 1 1 1 1 1 0 0 0 0 0 0 0 0	Mask

Network Address	Host

(b)

Fig. 7.5 Subnet Addressing

Actually some of these networks are divided into subnetworks, with part of the host number used to identify the subnetwork, as shown in Fig. 7.5(a). To identify subnetworks, routers maintain *subnet masks* in their routing tables, which are logically ANDed with the IP address, as shown in Fig. 7.5(b).

IP addresses can be described in printable strings by *domain literal* notation, with each octet represented by decimal number and separated by decimal points. For example: 191.47.22.8.

7.4.2 Routing

Although hosts do not forward datagrams, it is still necessary for the host to maintain some routing tables that contain the addresses of routers on the host's own network, "reachability" information through those routers, and certain other metrics. The tables maintained by multiple attached routers are more complicated, because they must be able to send a datagram on at least its next hop toward every network on the internet.

The two protocols that are most commonly used by internet routers are RIP and OSPF. RIP is based on a distance-vector algorithm and OSPF is based on a link-state algorithm. OSPF, which is gradually replacing RIP, allows networks to be organized into hierarchies, as shown in Fig. 7.6.

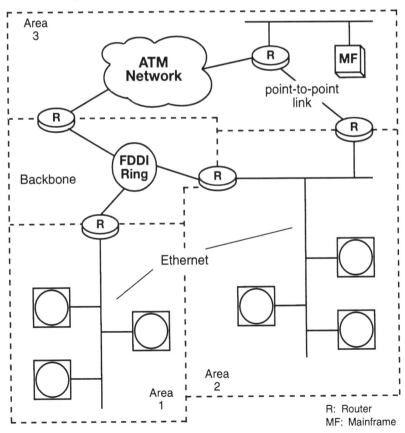

Fig. 7.6 Autonomous System

Fig. 7.6 shows an autonomous system—a network under a single administrative entity. Autonomous systems are subdivided into area networks, with a backbone network serving as a "hub." Within each area network OSPF functions normally. At area boundaries the situation is different, however. The link-state advertisements sent across area borders are limited to *summaries,* with routers only required to have detailed knowledge of the topology of their own area.

Routers on area borders are called *border routers.* They maintain complete routing tables of the network on either side of the border. Hub area routers are also considered border routers, if they are on an area border.

The OSPF hierarchy also includes *stub areas.* Stub areas only have one border router. Any datagram with a destination outside the stub area is automatically sent to the same exit point. Within a stub area no summary or external link-state advertisements circulate. They are not needed.

Problem Solving Example:

 How does the hierarchical organization of OSPF reduce the demands on network resources?

Since only reachability information is communicated across area boundaries, the computation of routing tables does not have to take into account the detailed topology of the entire autonomous system, just its own area. Also, since link-state advertisements that cross network boundaries are only summaries, network congestion is reduced.

7.4.3   The Internet Protocol (IP)

The best way to describe the Internet protocol is to describe the format of an IP datagram. First we will point out that what is contained in the data field of an IP datagram is usually an encapsulated TCP segment, or perhaps an encapsulated UDP datagram. If the TCP segment or the UDP datagram is too large, the source IP will *fragment* it, with the destination IP reassembling the fragments. Also, if allowed by the flag field of an IP header (see Fig. 7.7), the datagram may be fragmented at an intermediate node.

In some cases, the data field will contain an ICMP message, which also uses the IP delivery service.

1	5	9		17	20		32
Ver	IHL	TOS			Total Length		
Identification			FL		Fragment Offset		
Lifetime		Protocol			Header Checksum		
Source IP Address							
Destination IP Address							
Options • • •			• • •		Padding		
Data							

Fig. 7.7 IP Datagram

Fig. 7.7 shows the format of an IP datagram:

The fields of an IP datagram have the following significance:

1. **Version -** the version number of the IP. This is to allow for future evolution of the protocol.
2. **IHL: Internet Header Length -** This is the number of thirty-two bit words in the header. The minimum is five words, or twenty octets.
3. **TOS: Type of Service -** This includes reliability, precedence, delay, and throughput parameters.
4. **Total Length -** the total length of the header plus the data field in octets.
5. **Identification -** The unique identification of the datagram is a combination of this field, the source and destination address, and the user protocol. It is used to reassemble fragments.

6. **FL: Flags** - There are three bits in the flag field, two of which have been defined:
    - **More Bit** - used to indicate more fragments are to follow.
    - **Last Fragment** - indicates last fragment.
7. **Fragment Offset** - indicates the position, in units of eight octets, of the first octet of the fragment in the original datagram.
8. **Lifetime** - the maximum time a datagram has to reach its destination (in seconds). Each time the datagram is processed by the IP this field is decremented. Specifically this relates to the number of hops to live.
9. **Protocol** - identifies the upper layer protocol whose message is contained in the data field.
10. **Header Checksum** - a one's complement checksum computed over the header. This is recomputed at each hop.
11. **Source Address** - the IP address of the initial sender.
12. **Destination Address** - the IP address of the final destination.
13. **Option** - This is a variable field that specifies the options requested by the sender.
14. **Padding** - This field ensures that the IP datagram's header ends on a thirty-two bit boundary.
15. **Data** - The maximum length of this field is 65,535 (although usually much shorter) octets, and not necessarily a multiple of four octets.

If the datagram is an IP fragment, it is treated like any other datagram. The fragments are reassembled at the destination. When the first fragment arrives, the IP sets a timer. If not all of the fragments have arrived by the time the timer expires, or if one of them is corrupted, the entire datagram is discarded.

Obviously fragmenting can decrease throughput, since all it takes is for one of the fragments to be discarded (because of congestion at a router, for example), and the entire IP user's message must be retransmitted. We will explain more about why fragmenting is necessary in Section 7.5, The Interface Layer.

7.4.4 The Internet Control Message Protocol

If an anomaly occurs, the network nodes will exchange ICMP messages. ICMP messages are used to supervise and control the IP network. Actually, it is a very basic management protocol with more sophisticated network management performed by application layer protocols such as the Simple Network Management Protocol (SNMP).

The following are the ICMP messages:

1. **Destination Unreachable** - This means that a datagram was discarded because its destination was unknown, or because fragmenting was necessary for routing across a network, but not allowed by the flag field.
2. **Time Exceeded** - The datagram's lifetime had expired.
3. **Parameter Error** - indicates an illegal value in the header field—for example, an unknown protocol.
4. **Source Quench** - indicates a network node is discarding messages. An example would be a router with a shortage of buffers.
5. **Redirect** - used to report a router closer to the destination, or one that can route the message more efficiently.
6. **Echo Request** - used to test reachability of an IP address.
7. **Timestamp Request** - used to sample the delay between network devices.
8. **Information Request** - used to determine the address of the local IP network.
9. **Address-Mask Request** - used to determine the subnet-mask of the local IP network.
10. **Router Solicitation** - a tool provided for the discovery of routers.

7.5 The Interface Layer

An internet usually is made up of several different types of networks. Ethernet LANs and the X.25 WAN are the most common, but it may include one or more token ring LANs, or an FDDI backbone network, or others. The Internet consists of many different types of networks. It is the interface layer's responsibility to transmit a datagram between two IP network nodes, either of which may be a host or a router. If the sending network node is a router it may be attached to two or more different types of networks operating with different protocols.

The interface layer is equivalent to the data-link layer and the physical layer, but its responsibilities vary from network node to network node, depending upon what, if any, protocol conversion is necessary.

In a sense, however, the interface process is simpler than it sounds. If, for example, a datagram arrives at a router from an X.25 network and its destination is on an IEEE 802.3 shared bus, the interface entity on the 802.3 side does not have to worry about the X.25 protocol because that has been taken care of by the interface entity on the X.25 side. By the time it has reached the IP layer, and perhaps been reassembled from fragments, it is in the format of an IP datagram.

At this point, the IP datagram needs to be converted to a form that can be transmitted on a shared bus. The most straightforward way to do this is to encapsulate the datagram in an HDLC frame. Before the encapsulation can occur several issues need to be dealt with:

1. The IP address needs to be mapped to an IEEE 802.3 address. IP addresses are logical artifacts, while LAN addresses are physical artifacts—often hardwired into the device by the manufacturer. If the device is replaced, it might have a different physical address, but the same logical address (i.e., the same applications, database, and human users) from the view of the Internet and IP.
2. If the length of the datagram is less than 46 octets, padding needs to be added to bring it up to the 802.3 minimum.
3. If the length of the datagram is more than 1500 octets, the datagram needs to be fragmented. It is the interface layer's responsibility to inform the IP, which will perform the fragmenting, if it is permitted by the value in the flag field. For our example—the datagram arriving by way of an X.25 network—fragmentation would probably be permitted because the size of an X.25 packet is often about 128 bytes.

For an IEEE 802.3 network, address resolution is handled by the *address resolution protocol* (ARP). The ARP would check its *address cache*. If the shared bus address corresponding to the IP address was in the cache, it would inform the interface layer. If it was not, it would broadcast a special frame, shown in Fig. 7.8.

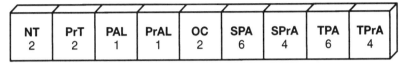

NT	PrT	PAL	PrAL	OC	SPA	SPrA	TPA	TPrA
2	2	1	1	2	6	4	6	4

Fig. 7.8 ARP Packet

The fields shown in the ARP frame (see Fig. 7.8) have the following significance:

1. **NT: Network Type -** CSMA/CD shared bus, otherwise known as Ethernet has an NT = 01.
2. **PrT: Protocol Type -** for the IP protocol, PrT = 0800.
3. **PAL: Physical Address Length -** CSMA/CD type of LANs usually have an address length of six octets.
4. **PrAL: Protocol Address Length -** The address length of the IP protocol is four octets.
5. **OC: Operation Code -** This is the code for an ARP address request.
6. **SPA: Sender Physical Address -** This is the physical address, as opposed to the logical IP address, of the router on the CSMA/CD LAN.
7. **SPrA: Sender Protocol Address -** This is the IP address of the router.
8. **TPA: Target Physical Address -** This is the physical address that the ARP is attempting to obtain. This field is left blank.
9. **TPrA: Target Protocol Address -** This field contains 4 octets for an IP address. This address is already known to the sender.

The operation code used by ARP would be 01. The only field not filled in would be the target physical address. Of course, the ARP packet would be encapsulated in an 802.3 frame. When the destination system responded with the physical address, the ARP would add it to its cache and inform the interface layer. The interface layer would then transmit a frame containing the datagram to the destination. Actually, the frame would be the result of two encapsulations: (1) the IP datagram in an LLC PDU, with the source address being 06, for the TCP environment (see Fig. 5.3 on page 124), and (2) the LLC PDU in a MAC frame.

IP is a connectionless protocol, but sometimes it must be interfaced with a connection-oriented network. When this occurs, it is the interface layer's responsibility to establish a connection prior to forwarding the datagram on the physical network.

Problem Solving Example:

How does the interface layer transmit a datagram across an Ethernet?

It encapsulates the datagram in a MAC frame. The interface layer knows the datagram will not be too large, because IP will have fragmented it, if necessary. The translation from the destination IP address to the destination MAC address is achieved using the address resolution protocol (ARP).

7.6 The Next Generation of the Internet Protocol (IPv6)

To the engineers who developed IP Version 4 in 1975 the desktop PC was no more than a futuristic concept. PCs are now commonplace, and the result is a demand for Internet services that has pushed IPv4 to its limit.

In some ways network administrators have been able to adapt. For example, private intranets often use address space already allocated on the Internet, relying on network address translators (NATs) to intercept Internet traffic, performing needed address conversion. In other ways, such as providing services that IPv4 was not designed for (e.g., real time video), there is not much that can be done to improve quality.

It has become increasingly clear that it is time to phase in a new protocol that will take the Internet into the next century. To accomplish this the Internet Engineering Task Force (IETF) first designed a simpler, slimmed down IP packet. Some of the fields of the IPv4 datagram have been discarded, while others have been aligned with 32-bits. The most striking change made to the IPv6 datagram is the expansion of the source and destination address fields to 128-bits, as shown in Fig. 7.9.

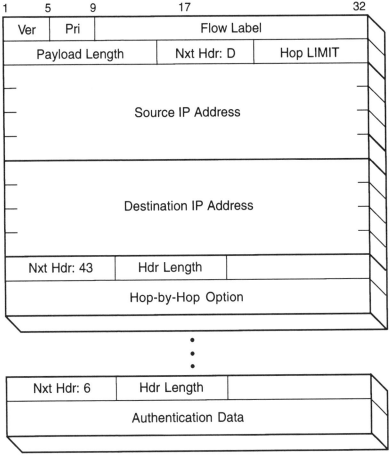

Fig. 7.9 IPv6 Datagram

An interesting point about IPv6 addresses is that they are automatically derivable from the unique 48-bit NIC addresses. This was planned to allow new IPv6 hosts to auto-configure, avoiding the task of manually configuring adds to large networks.

The size of the address fields, 128-bits, may seem like a lot, but, at first, so did the 32-bit IPv4 address fields. In theory IPv4 allowed for 4 billion unique addresses. But it turned out that the Internet ran out of class B networks. This was because a lot of class B space was wasted by allocating addresses to networks with only about 300 hosts (vs. the maximum of 65,536). This time around, the IETF wanted to ensure a hierarchical address structure that would last a long time, thus 128-bit addresses were selected.

The significance of the fields of the IPv6 datagrams are as follows:

1. Version: 6 goes here.
2. Priority: There are two broad categories of priority: congestion controlled (0-7), and non- congestion controlled (8-15). Congestion controlled values indicate that the source host will slow the transmission to alleviate congestion. On the other hand, hosts running real-time applications, which are more delay sensitive, are usually non-congestion controlled. The 8-15 priority levels are not actually higher than the 0-7, they are just different categories. Real time audio will often transmit with alternating higher and lower priority datagrams (e.g., 10 and 11), because algorithms usually allow recovery from a single packet loss (at a time of congestion, two alternating 10s would be discarded first, while two alternating 11s would hopefully go through).
3. Flow Label: This 24-bit field is chosen by the source host. All of the datagrams in the same flow must have the same options and header extensions (see 5), and the same destination. This allows a router to process the first datagram in a flow, and to rapidly forward those that follow. A router will time out on a flow after 6 seconds, so flows sometimes have to be re-established.

4. Payload Length: The length of the IP datagram, minus the basic header. The maximum length is 16,535 bytes, unless the jumbo option is selected in the hop- by-hop options (see 5. below).

5. Next Header: This field is the equivalent of the options field in the IPv4 datagram, but it is more efficient because routers do not need to review all the options. The value contained in this field identifies the extension header that follows, with every extension header having its own Next Header field (see Fig. 7.9):

    - 0: Hop-by-Hop options: Every router must process this header. There are three options, one padding byte, N padding bytes, and jumbo payload length (greater than 16535 bytes).

    - 43: Routing Information: This extension header allows the source host to designate the exact route, or a loose route.

    - 44: Fragment Identification: Contains the fragment ID, offset, and the more bit. Different from IPv4 fragmentation in that only the source host can fragment a datagram.

    - 6: Authentication: Security - IPv4 had no way of providing authentication, or confidentiality, except at the application level. IPv6 provides both by means of encryption keys.

6. Hop Limit: Same as the time to live field in IPv4. Routers decrement this field on each hop until it reaches zero. Then the datagram is discarded to preventing looping.

7. Source Address: The address of the source host.

8. Destination Address: The address of the destination host. IPv6 provides multicast addressing for destination addresses that begin with a 16-bit 3333.

The migration to IPv6 is being made easier by tunneling: embedding IPv6 packets in IPv4 datagrams. This allows two IPv6 hosts to communicate, even if they are separated by an IPv4 network. Other transition facilitating techniques include systems that maintain dual IPv4 and IPv6 stacks, and devices that function as translators between the two versions.

7.7 Service Primitives

Like other protocols, the TCP/IP standards specify services in the form of service primitives, which are functional specifications—leaving the implementation up to the vendor. For example, IP responds to the SEND primitive, which is usually a request from TCP, by sending a datagram. The destination IP informs the destination protocol, usually TCP, with the DELIVER primitive. Both the SEND and the DELIVER primitives have about eight parameters.

7.8 Data Representation by the Simple Network Management Protocol (SNMP)

How data is represented internally, by a device that implements TCP/IP, is generally not a major concern as long as the PDU header fields conform to the big endian format. The TCP and UDP protocols provide a transparent data service for the application layer. Since the data is transparent to the entities below the application layer, how the data is represented, or is interpreted, doesn't affect the TCP/IP protocols of the lower four layers.

At the application level the issue of data representation is more significant. Application peer entities must be able to interpret each others data. How data is represented in memory—by applications on different computers—depends on: 1. the machine architecture, 2. the operating system, 3. the application programming language, and 4. the compiler chosen for that language. On some systems a C language integer is 16 bits. On others, it is 32 bits. Also, the internal format of more complex data structures, such as arrays, may vary even if the representation of individual components is the same.

The Simple Network Management Protocol (SNMP) is a TCP/IP protocol that offers network management service for the application layer. SNMP maintains a data base of the management framework: the *management information base* (MIB). The MIB is distributed on all nodes that make up the network managed by SNMP (in most cases, either a proprietary network or an autonomous system). In order to insure consistent data representation, SNMP has borrowed Abstract Syntax Notation One (ASN.1) from the OSI Model's presentation layer, and made it available to define the MIB.

7.8.1 Abstract Syntax and Transfer Syntax Pairs

Abstract syntaxes are intended to be paired with one or more transfer syntax. In the case of SNMP there is only one pair of interest: ASN.1 and *Basic Encoding Rules* (BER); both will be briefly described.

7.8.2 Abstract Syntax Notation One (ASN.1)

A type and a *value* of that type are defined below. Note that the ASN.1 word for variable is value.

```
TypeName ::= TYPE
valueName TypeName ::= VALUE
```

By convention, ASN.1 reserved words are upper case, type names begin with capital letters, and value names begin with lower case letters. ASN.1 also allows possible values to be associated with symbolic names when a type is defined, for example:

```
Access ::= INTEGER { none (0), partial (1), unlimited (2) }
userAccess Access ::= partial
- userAccess equals 1
```

Since Access is defined to be an INTEGER type, userAccess is an integer value. An ASN.1 integer value can be any cardinal number, with its size (the number of bits) determined by the number assigned to it. Note, from the above, that comments are preceded by a double dash '--'.

The *bit string* type allows the user to declare one or more named bits:

```
Status BIT STRING ::= { operational (1), down (0), new (1) }
deviceStatus Status ::= { operational, new } - equals '11'B
```

OCTET STRING types are defined in a way similar to bit string types, except named octets are defined instead of named bits.

The are two kinds of ASN.1 types, primitive types and *constructed* types. The ones we've discussed so far are primitive types. The *sequence* type, which is similar to a C structure, is a constructed type.

```
WorkStation ::= SEQUENCE
        {
            operatorAccess Access,
            desktopStatus Status
        }
```

SEQUENCE OF types are defined in a way similar to sequences, except every element must be the same ASN.1 type. A good analogy for the SEQUENCE OF is the dynamic array.

Since the defined length of primitive types is virtually unlimited, and since the fields of SEQUENCE and SEQUENCE OF types may be any valid type, including constructed types, just about any data structure may be defined. And even for a few unusual cases, the ASN.1 macro type can be used to modify the rules. Table 7.2 lists some well-known ASN.1 types.

ASN.1 TYPE	Universal Tag
BOOLEAN	1
INTEGER	2
BIT STRING	3
OCTET STRING	4
NULL	5
OBJECT IDENTIFIER	6
Object Descriptor	7
EXTERNAL	8
REAL	9
ENUMERATED	10
SEQUENCE OF, SEQUENCE	16
SET OF, SET	17
Character String	28

Table 7.2 Abstract Syntax Notation One—Commonly Used Types and Corresponding Universal Tags

7.8.3 Basic Encoding Rules (BER)

The *universal tags* shown in Table 7.2 are used with the transfer syntax, BER, to identify well-known ASN.1 data types. In addition to universal tags, there are three user defined *tag classes*, as shown in Table 7.3. Examples of the other tag classes will not be presented, but basically the way it works is that the programmer identifies "tags," a user defined type by simply including an integer—one that is unique within the type's scope—as part of the type definition. The tag can then be used to identify any value defined to be of that type when the transfer syntax, BER, is applied. Examples of BER, including its use of the tag field, will be presented.

Tag Class	Description	Bits 7 & 8 of Tag Field
Universal	Well-known ASN.1 types.	00
Application-Wide	Must be unique within an ASN.1 Module.	01
Context-Specific	Must be unique within an ASN.1 Module.	10
Private-Use	Unique within a given enterprise.	11

Table 7.3 ASN.1 Tag Classes

According to the BER, ASN.1 values are encoded in three fields: the *tag field*, the *length field*, and the *contents field*, as shown in Figure 7.10(a).

Tag	Length	Value

(a) BER Fields Used to Encode ASN.1 Values

(Fig. 7.10 continued on next page)

(Fig. 7.10 continued from previous page)

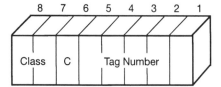

C: constructed bit

(b) First Byte of Tag Field

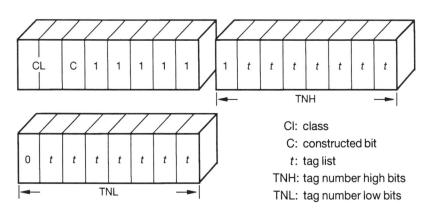

CI: class
C: constructed bit
t: tag list
TNH: tag number high bits
TNL: tag number low bits

(c) Three Byte Encoding of Tag Field

Fig. 7.10 ASN.1 and Tag Field Encoding

The first two bits of the tag field are used to identify the tag class (see Table 7.3 and Figure 7.10(b)). The third bit is used to indicate a constructed type. The five least significant bits are used to encode the tag number, if it is less than 31. (Note: all of the universal tags are less than 31.) If the tag is too large to be encoded in five bits, then all five bits are set to 1, and at least one additional byte is required. After the first byte, the high-order bit is used to indicate if this is the last byte of the tag field (see Figure 7.10(c)).

If the high-order bit of the first byte of the length field is a 1, than the number of bytes required for the length is stored in the lower seven bits (see Figure 7.11(a) on the next page). If the high-order bit of the first byte of the length field is a 0, than the length is stored in the lower seven bits (see Figure 7.11(b)).

An integer is always encoded as a primitive type (see Figure 7.11(b)). The number of bytes of the contents field is determined by

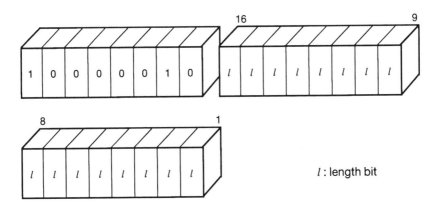

(a) Three Byte Encoding of Length

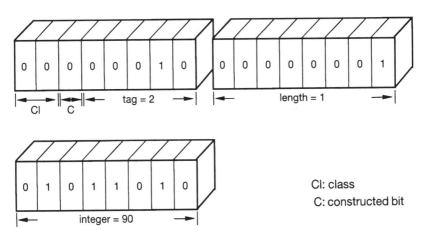

(b) Encoding of Integer

(Fig. 7.11 continued on next page)

(Fig. 7.11 continued from previous page)

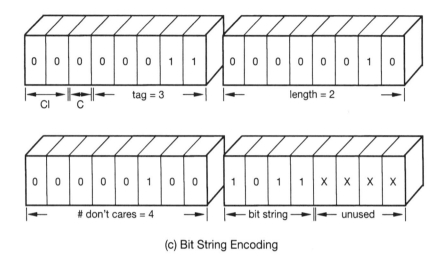

(c) Bit String Encoding

Fig. 7.11   BER Encoding of Length, Integer Type, and Bit String Type

the length field. The integer's value is stored in the contents field in two's compliment form.

BER allows a bit string to be encoded either as a primitive type, or as a constructed type. However, this discussion concentrates on the primitive case, because SNMP does not allow non-primitive bit strings. The length field contains the number of bytes needed to hold the bit string, plus one. This allows for a "don't care" byte that comes first in the contents field. The "don't care" byte contains the number of don't care bits, if any, in the last byte of the contents field (see Figure 7.11(c)). The last byte will have some don't cares, if the bit string is not evenly divisible by eight.

Encoding Constructed Types According to BER

Constructed types, such as the SEQUENCE and SEQUENCE OF types are encoded in the SNMP environment by first computing the length, then recursively applying the BER to each element.

7.9 Other Internet Protocols

Real Time Protocol (RTP)

The real time protocol (RTP) was developed for real-time applications such as video conferencing and real-time audio. It was designed to work with UDP to give the application program maximum timing control. TCP insures the reliable in-sequence delivery of data, but it has the disadvantage that the delivery is sometimes held up while packets are resequenced, or retransmissions are requested.

Often real-time applications are better off estimating what would have been sent. For example, a video application might freeze on a frame waiting for a retransmission, when an estimate would only cause a small amount of fuzziness.

RTP can work with the resource reservation protocol (RRSP) to reserve network resources for required throughput.

7.9.1 Interdomain Routing Protocol (IDRP)

RIP and OSPF are interior gateway protocols. Interdomain routing protocol (IDRP) is an exterior gateway protocol whose purpose is to provide routing between autonomous systems. IDRP supports routing between "confederations," which are groups of autonomous systems.

7.9.2 Point-to-Point Protocol

The point-to-point protocol (PPP) is used to route IP datagrams across a direct link (see Fig. 7.6). IP datagrams are usually routed across networks, and the data-link protocol of that network is utilized by the interface layer. But sometimes only a point-to-point link is available, so PPP provides the data-link layer service. PPP is similar in structure to LLC.

Point-to-point links may include ISDN connections, T1 carriers, or microwave links.

The serial line interface protocol (SLIP) is another TCP/IP protocol used for direct links.

Problem Solving Example:

Why has the real time protocol (RTP) been developed? Why does it use the RSRP?

The original TCP/IP suite was not intended for isochronous time-sensitive data such as audio or video. RTP focuses on these new kinds of network traffic. RTP works in conjunction with the resource reservation protocol (RSRP) in order to reserve the necessary resources to avoid packet delays. For example, if an internet has a 51.84 mbps access to an ATM network, RSRP may reserve 6 mbps; this would be appropriate for a video-conferencing application.

List of Acronyms

AAL	ATM Adaption layer	**BPRZ-AMI**	Bipolar Return-to-Zero Alternate Mark Inversion
ADSL	Asymmetric Digital Subscriber Line	**BSD**	Berkeley Software Distribution
ANSI	American National Standards Institute	**BSD-UNIX**	Berkeley Software Distribution Unix Operating System
ARPA	Advanced Research Project Agency	**CBR**	Constant Bit Rate
ARPANET	Advanced Research Project Agency Network	**CRC**	Cyclical Redundancy Check
		CS	Convergence Sublayer
ASCII	American Standard Code for Information Interchange	**CSMA/CD**	Carrier Sense Multiple Access/ Collision Detection
ATM	Asynchronous Transfer Mode	**DCE**	Data Circuit Terminating Equipment
AUI	Attachment Unit Interface	**DCS**	Defined Context Set
BECN	Backward Explicit Congestion Notification	**DDS**	Dataphone Digital Service or Digital Data Service

DQDB	Dual Queue Dual Bus	**IEEE**	Institute of Electrical and Electronics Engineers
DSU/CSU	Digital Service Unit/Channel Service Unit	**IETF**	Internet Engineering Task Force
DTE	Data Terminal Equipment	**IP**	Internet Protocol
DXI	Data Exchange Interface	**ISDN**	Integrated Services Digital Network
EBCDIC	Extended Binary Coded Decimal Interchange Code	**ISO**	International Organization for Standardization
FCS	Frame Check Sequence	**ISO/OSI**	International Organization for Standardization/ Open Systems Interconnection
FDDI	Fiber Distributed Data Interface		
FECN	Forward Explicit Congestion Notification	**ITU-T**	International Telecommunication Union — Telecommunication Standardization Sector
FM	Frequency Modulation		
GFC	Generic Flow Control		
HDLC	High-Level Data Link Control	**LAN**	Local Area Network
HDSL	High Bit Rate Digital Subscriber Line	**LAP-B**	Link Access Protocol Balanced
		LCN	Logical Channel Number
IANA	Internet Assigned Names Authority	**LED**	Light Emitting Diode
ICMP	Internet Control Message Protocol	**LLC**	Logical Link Control
IDRP	Interdomain Routing Protocol	**MAC**	Medium Access Control

MAN	Metropolitan Area Network	**PVC**	Permanent Virtual Circuit
MII	Medium Independent Interface	**QAM**	Quadrature Amplitude Modulation
MILNET	Military Network		
NIC	Network Interface Card	**QOS**	Quality of Service
NNI	Network Node Interface	**RIP**	Routing Information Protocol
NRZI	Non-Return to Zero Inverted	**RTP**	Real Time Protocol
NSFNET	National Science Foundation Network	**SAP**	Service Access Point
		SAR	Segmentation and Reassembly
OSI	Open Systems Interconnection	**SDLC**	Synchronous Data Link Control
OSPF	Open Shortest Path First	**SDU**	Service Data Unit
		SMDS	Switched Multi-Megabit Digital Service
PAD	Packet Assembler Disassembler		
PC	Personal Computer	**SNA**	System Network Architecture
PCI	Protocol Control Information	**SONET**	Synchronous Optical Network
PCM	Pulse Code Modulation	**SVC**	Signalling Virtual Channel
PDU	Protocol Data Unit	**TCP**	Transmission Control Protocol
PM	Phase Modulation		
POP	Port of Presence	**TCP/IP**	Transmission Control Protocol/ Internet Protocol
PPP	Point-to-Point Protocol		
PRI	Primary Rate Interface	**TCM**	Trellis-Coded Modulation

TDM	Time Division Modulation
TIA/EIA	Telecommunications Industries Association/ Electronic Industries Association
TTRT	Target Token Rotation Time
UDP	User Datagram Protocol
UNI	User Node Interface
VBR	Variable Bit Rate
VC	Virtual Channel or Virtual Connection
VCI	Virtual Channel Identifier
VCN	Virtual Channel Number
VPI	Virtual Path Identifier
WAN	Wide Area Network

Unit Abbreviations

ABBREVIATIONS	UNITS REPRESENTED
m	meters
s	seconds
ms	milliseconds
Hz	Hertz
kbps	kilobits per second
mbps	megabits per second
gbps	gigabits per second
kBaud	kiloBaud
Mbaud	MegaBaud
kHz	kiloHertz
MHz	MegaHertz
gHz	GigaHertz

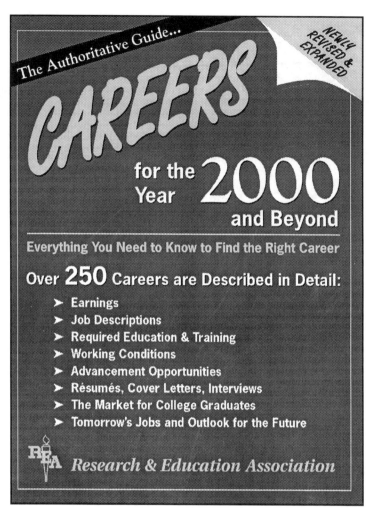

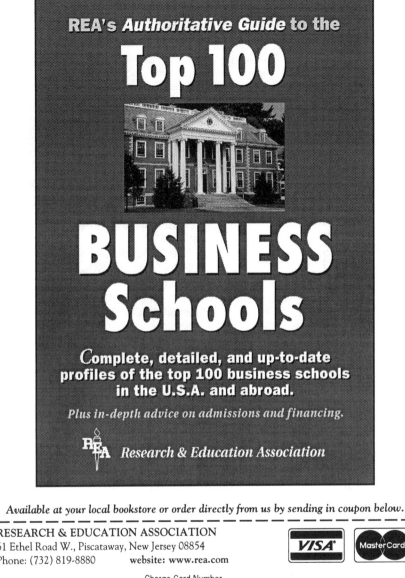

REA's **Problem Solvers**

The "PROBLEM SOLVERS" are comprehensive supplemental text-books designed to save time in finding solutions to problems. Each "PROBLEM SOLVER" is the first of its kind ever produced in its field. It is the product of a massive effort to illustrate almost any imaginable problem in exceptional depth, detail, and clarity. Each problem is worked out in detail with a step-by-step solution, and the problems are arranged in order of complexity from elementary to advanced. Each book is fully indexed for locating problems rapidly.

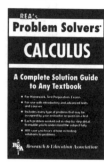

ACCOUNTING
ADVANCED CALCULUS
ALGEBRA & TRIGONOMETRY
AUTOMATIC CONTROL
   SYSTEMS/ROBOTICS
BIOLOGY
BUSINESS, ACCOUNTING, & FINANCE
CALCULUS
CHEMISTRY
COMPLEX VARIABLES
DIFFERENTIAL EQUATIONS
ECONOMICS
ELECTRICAL MACHINES
ELECTRIC CIRCUITS
ELECTROMAGNETICS
ELECTRONIC COMMUNICATIONS
ELECTRONICS
FINITE & DISCRETE MATH
FLUID MECHANICS/DYNAMICS
GENETICS
GEOMETRY
HEAT TRANSFER

LINEAR ALGEBRA
MACHINE DESIGN
MATHEMATICS for ENGINEERS
MECHANICS
NUMERICAL ANALYSIS
OPERATIONS RESEARCH
OPTICS
ORGANIC CHEMISTRY
PHYSICAL CHEMISTRY
PHYSICS
PRE-CALCULUS
PROBABILITY
PSYCHOLOGY
STATISTICS
STRENGTH OF MATERIALS &
   MECHANICS OF SOLIDS
TECHNICAL DESIGN GRAPHICS
THERMODYNAMICS
TOPOLOGY
TRANSPORT PHENOMENA
VECTOR ANALYSIS

*If you would like more information about any of these books,
complete the coupon below and return it to us or visit your local bookstore.*

RESEARCH & EDUCATION ASSOCIATION
61 Ethel Road W. • Piscataway, New Jersey 08854
Phone: (732) 819-8880   **website: www.rea.com**

Please send me more information about your Problem Solver books

Name _____

Address _____

City _____ State _____ Zip _____

"The ESSENTIALS" of HISTORY

REA's **Essentials of History** series offers a new approach to the study of history that is different from what has been available previously. Compared with conventional history outlines, the **Essentials of History** offer far more detail, with fuller explanations and interpretations of historical events and developments. Compared with voluminous historical tomes and textbooks, the **Essentials of History** offer a far more concise, less ponderous overview of each of the periods they cover.

The **Essentials of History** provide quick access to needed information, and will serve as handy reference sources at all times. The **Essentials of History** are prepared with REA's customary concern for high professional quality and student needs.

UNITED STATES HISTORY

1500 to 1789 From Colony to Republic
1789 to 1841 The Developing Nation
1841 to 1877 Westward Expansion & the Civil War
1877 to 1912 Industrialism, Foreign Expansion & the Progressive Era
1912 to 1941 World War I, the Depression & the New Deal
America since 1941: Emergence as a World Power

EUROPEAN HISTORY

1450 to 1648 The Renaissance, Reformation & Wars of Religion
1648 to 1789 Bourbon, Baroque & the Enlightenment
1789 to 1848 Revolution & the New European Order
1848 to 1914 Realism & Materialism
1914 to 1935 World War I & Europe in Crisis
Europe since 1935: From World War II to the Demise of Communism

WORLD HISTORY

Ancient History (4500 BC to AD 500) The Emergence of Western Civilization
Medieval History (AD 500 to 1450) The Middle Ages

CANADIAN HISTORY

Pre-Colonization to 1867 The Beginning of a Nation
1867 to Present The Post-Confederate Nation

If you would like more information about any of these books, complete the coupon below and return it to us or visit your local bookstore.

RESEARCH & EDUCATION ASSOCIATION
61 Ethel Road W. • Piscataway, New Jersey 08854
Phone: (732) 819-8880   **website: www.rea.com**

Please send me more information about your History Essentials books

Name _____

Address _____

City _____ State _____ Zip _____

REA's Test Preps
The Best in Test Preparation

- REA "Test Preps" are **far more** comprehensive than any other test preparation series
- Each book contains up to **eight** full-length practice tests based on the most recent exams
- **Every** type of question likely to be given on the exams is included
- Answers are accompanied by **full** and **detailed** explanations

REA has published over 60 Test Preparation volumes in several series. They include:

Advanced Placement Exams (APs)
Biology
Calculus AB & Calculus BC
Chemistry
Computer Science
English Language & Composition
English Literature & Composition
European History
Government & Politics
Physics
Psychology
Statistics
Spanish Language
United States History

College-Level Examination Program (CLEP)
Analyzing and Interpreting Literature
College Algebra
Freshman College Composition
General Examinations
General Examinations Review
History of the United States I
Human Growth and Development
Introductory Sociology
Principles of Marketing
Spanish

SAT II: Subject Tests
American History
Biology E/M
Chemistry
English Language Proficiency Test
French
German

SAT II: Subject Tests (cont'd)
Literature
Mathematics Level IC, IIC
Physics
Spanish
Writing

Graduate Record Exams (GREs)
Biology
Chemistry
Computer Science
Economics
Engineering
General
History
Literature in English
Mathematics
Physics
Psychology
Sociology

ACT - ACT Assessment

ASVAB - Armed Services Vocational Aptitude Battery

CBEST - California Basic Educational Skills Test

CDL - Commercial Driver License Exam

CLAST - College-Level Academic Skills Test

ELM - Entry Level Mathematics

ExCET - Exam for the Certification of Educators in Texas

FE (EIT) - Fundamentals of Engineering Exam

FE Review - Fundamentals of Engineering Review

GED - High School Equivalency Diploma Exam (U.S. & Canadian editions)

GMAT - Graduate Management Admission Test

LSAT - Law School Admission Test

MAT - Miller Analogies Test

MCAT - Medical College Admission Test

MSAT - Multiple Subjects Assessment for Teachers

NJ HSPT - New Jersey High School Proficiency Test

PPST - Pre-Professional Skills Tests

PRAXIS II/NTE - Core Battery

PSAT - Preliminary Scholastic Assessment Test

SAT I - Reasoning Test

SAT I - Quick Study & Review

TASP - Texas Academic Skills Program

TOEFL - Test of English as a Foreign Language

TOEIC - Test of English for International Communication

RESEARCH & EDUCATION ASSOCIATION
61 Ethel Road W. • Piscataway, New Jersey 08854
Phone: (732) 819-8880   **website: www.rea.com**

Please send me more information about your Test Prep books

Name _____

Address _____

City _____ State _____ Zip _____